ART AND CULTURE OF MARGINALISED NOMADIC TRIBES IN ANDHRA PRADESH

ART AND CULTURE OF MARGINALISED NOMADIC TRIBES IN ANDHRA PRADESH

P. SADANANDAM

GYAN PUBLISHING HOUSE

NEW DELHI-110002

The Publication of this book has been financially supported by the Indian Council of Historical Research. The Responsibility for the facts stated or opinions expressed is entirely of the author and not of the council.

Art and Culture of Marginalised Nomadic Tribes in Andhra Pradesh

ISBN: 81-212-0958-7

Published in 2008 in India by
Gyan Publishing House
5, Ansari Road, Darya Ganj,
New Delhi-110002
Phones : 23282060, 23261060
Fax : 011-23285914
E-mail : books@ gyanbooks.com
Website: www.gyanbooks.com

Lassertype Setting by: Rudra Computer Graphics
Printed at : Singhal Print Media, Delhi

To

My Parents

Sri. P. Agaiah and Smt. P. Laxmi

Contents

Preface

The Indian sub-continent or Bharatakhanda, from Himalayas to Cape Kanyakumari forming a holy 'Inverted Triangle', is a world by itself. This land, now known as South Asia in Western academic parlance, is not a 'museum' of cultures. It is in reality an abode of living communities of diverse cultures evolving to perfection, sharing the natural and physical resources without mutual conflicts from times immemorial. The rich diversity in ethnic cultures exhibits a very wide range, from anthropological to highly spiritual. Simple living, non-exploitative means of livelihood, well organized family life, strong filial commitments, spirit of sacrifice, quest for life beyond death and overall attitudes of self reliance and self respect are some of the basic characteristics common to all Indian communities – tribal, semi-tribal or marginal and civilised. The customs, traditions and beliefs of these communities are based on the faith that they all hail from One and the same origin which they might prefer to identify with one or the other cosmic or natural phenomenon. From the tribal communities' unquestioning belief in the existence of Supreme Power to the highly speculative and philosophical thought of Brahman as reflected in the Vedanta, the Indian psyche could be understood as reflecting various dimensions of a common theme. This common psyche perhaps enabled various communities to live in peace and exchange their cultural traits for mutual benefit.

This South Asia Region now politically divided into seven independent States (known as SARC countries) can boast of a unique status for its unbroken and ever expanding civilization backed by a very high Culture. The beginnings of this Cultured civilization can not however be traced historically. However, the secret of its continuity could be understood from its nature of peaceful assimilation of diverse cultural trends in its main stream without dissolving their cultural identities. Thus, a solid cultural mosaic has formed in this Region with the voluntary participation of all cultures— classical, folk or tribal. The arts and crafts of 'little' or 'great' traditions have equally enriched the civilization and culture of this land.

Studies in Indian folklore reveal cultural assimilation while preserving the sensitivities of various 'little' traditions. The sincere efforts of the ancient sages to reach out to the masses could be found in the development of folk arts for enlightenment through entertainment. While the Vedanta and Sastras were meant to serve the intellectual class, the Puranas were written for the benefit of common man. These Puranas are not lesser on any count than the Vedic literature. They are popular histories and each one of the major Purana is an encyclopedia by itself. Thus they are the storehouses of knowledge. They impart education, propagate Dharma and teach wisdom to all sections of people from a common platform. This effort has been continuously pursued by the 'great' tradition to help grow the 'little' while preserving their typical characteristics and art forms.

The Puranas are followed by the Epics which constituted major content of the folk art performances. Buddhist and Jain traditions also attempted to reach the common man in the contemporary folk languages. Dharma has been the under-current of all these literary and art forms, both classical and folk. Sathguru Sivananda Murty, D.Lit. (Bheemunipatnam, A.P.) while explaining the phenomenon in his simple and truth-revealing words, says that the Supreme Intelligence descends in myriad forms to help the ascent of man. This is also symbolically presented as a "Triangle in an Inverted Triangle" in the Vedic-lore. Thus the classical knowledge and folk art forms were integrated to facilitate the 'Cultural Osmosis'. The diminishing number of tribes and tribal population in India from the remotest past to the present could mainly be ascribed to this natural process. As civilization became widespread, many hill-tribes and forest communities were naturally attracted to join the main stream. The development of modern vernaculars in medieval times has further hastened this process of assimilation. For, select folk art forms are employed to preserve the pride and culture of each community through their own historical narratives describing their origins to confirm that they were branched out of the same stem.

The holistic and all inclusive character of the 'great' tradition was considered a major threat to the invading armies and alien cultures. Modern European colonists resorted to brutal annihilation of aboriginal tribes and native cultures in Americas and Australia. The English had applied persuasive methods of conversion of masses to Western culture and religion in South Asia. Two centuries of British rule developed many a crack in the Indian Cultural Mosaic. 'Leave them alone' policy of the 'Raj' in respect of tribal communities stalled the process of assimilation and the gaps were, thus, widened. And the post independent era has further widened the cleavages. The rich diversity, which was once a uniting force, has turned out to be the weakness of Indian culture. The smaller units have become mutually antagonistic and collectively defiant to the uniting spirit of the age-old Culture. To assuage the wounds inflicted by the British Imperialists on Indian culture and civilization, the truth-seeking historians have to work with due seriousness to take up studies based on Indian folklore which is 'live' historical data.

The folk arts were so popular that each family could boast of its own custom and tradition with pride and every community was patronizing its own peculiar art forms by dedicating some of their families as 'conservators' of their history. 'Andhra-desa' which was bubbling with numerous folk arts served as a link between north and south Indian patterns. The folk arts are so integrated with the classical Pan-Indian art that the former serve as roots and branches of the latter. The 'cultural tsunami' of the West, with its typical imperialist force, has swept away the native 'little' traditions which illuminated the earlier times through the generations. Now one or two small lamps representing them may be found flickering here and there. In the recent times, some efforts are made by the scholars and institutions to record and document these folk forms which are fast fading. There is a need to study these art forms from a historical perspective to enlighten and educate the future generations on the human values for which those cultures stood. The present work attempts to serve this purpose.

I congratulate Dr P. Sadanandam for presenting his studious research work in a lucid style. May the Almighty bless him with long life in perfect health backed by all resources to continue his academic research in this direction!

United States, Dallas, TX,
July 8, 2007 —— *Y. Sudershan Rao*

Acknowledgements

At this eventful moment in my life, I deem it a pleasant duty to express my utmost reverence salutations to my Guru Pujya Sri Sivananda Murty garu, Bheemunipatnam for his constant love and care.

I take this opportunity to express my sincere and immense gratitude to my teacher and research supervisor, Prof. Y. Sudershan Rao, Dean, Faculty of Social Sciences, Kakatiya University for his kind guidance throughout my academic career and life with lots of affection and care. But for his scholarly guidance and meticulous care, the work would not have assumed the present form.

I cordially express my sincere gratitudes to Smt. Y. Sharada Sudershan Rao and their daughters Hema Pramod, Sandhya and Sushama for their affection and encouragement throughout.

I owe my sincere thanks to Indian Council of Historical Research, New Delhi for awarding me Junior Research Fellowship (1995-1997) for my Research work.

I shall be failing in my duty if I do not acknowledge the goodwill of the authorities of the A.P. State Archives, Hyderabad ; the Directorate of Archaeology and Museums and American studies

Research centre, Hyderabad; Osmania University Library, Hyderabad; State Central Library, Hyderabad; School of Folk and Tribal Lore, Potti Sri Ramulu Telugu University, Orugallu campus, Warangal and various libraries and institutions who have readily agreed to my request for permission to consult the records and to collect relevant material. I also acknowledge my debt to the Nomadic Tribes who had patiently responded to my structured and open-ended questionnaires.

I am grateful to Dr. P. Hymavathi, Head, Department of History, and Dr. L. Vidyasagar Reddy, Chairmen, Board of studies, Department of History, Kakatiya University, Warangal for thier encouragement.

I am also thankful to Dr. A. Bobbili, Associate professor, Dr. Syed Ayub Ali, Associate professor, of the Department of History, Kakatiya University ; Sri. G. Bhadru Naik, Incharge Head, Department of History, University Arts and Science college, Warangal for their co-operation and encouragement.

I am very much beholden to Prof. P. Mallikarjuna Rao, Dean, Faculty of Arts; Prof. Hari Shiva Kumar, Department of Telugu, of Kakatiya University, Warangal for their valuable suggestions. I also owe my gratitude to Dr. C. Madan Mohan, Reader in Pub. Admn ; Dr. D. Swadesh, Reader in History of L.B. College, Warangal and Dr. G. Meeneshwar Rao, Reader in History, C.K.M. College, Warangal who have been my constant source of inspiration.

I wish to express my sincere thanks to Prof. N. Bhakthavathsala Reddy, Dean, School of Folk and Tribal Lore, Potti Sri Ramulu Telugu University, Orugallu campus, Warangal for his friendly co-operation and necessary help who provided me the most valuable photographs of Nomadic Tribes, particularly Sadanasurulu, Patam Chakallu, Chindus and material with regard to my research work. But for his constant help the work would not have been completed.

I am grateful to Dr. V. Gopal Reddy, Principal, Dr. M. Swamy, Vice-Principal University Arts and Science College, Subedari, Warangal for their kind encouragement.

I am specially thankful to my friend Mr. K. Vijaya Babu, Asst. Prof., Department of History, Kakatiya University, Warangal for his inspiring encouragement and interest which helped me in the successful completion of my dissertation. His perceptive and analytical remarks on different chapters contributed for the enrichment of the thesis.

At this occation of happiness, I wish to remember the co-operation and encouragement extended by my wife Umadevi and my children Humani Sucharitha, Sujan, Jyothi and other family members Smt. Radha, Sri. Upender, Mr. K. Rajender, Anasurya, Krishnaveni and Ganesh.

I am thankful to Mr. T. Buchi Babu, Correspondent, Bharati Vidya Bhavan, Hanamkonda for his encouragement. I am also thankful to Dr. J. Madhukar, President and Mr.Ch. Srinivas, General Secretary, KUPTA for their encouragement. I am thankful to Dr. Raj Mahammad, Teacher for his suggetions.

At this hour of satisfaction, I should like to remember my friends sarvasri Dr.T. Dayakar Rao, M. Sambaiah, Dr. G. Yadava Reddy, B. Mallesham, B. Sambamurthy, T. Brahmam, G. Venkanna, Anjaiah, Dr. Ramesh Reddy, Venkataramana, Kanakaratnam, T. Manohar for their constant encouragement and help. I also thank Sri. K. Surender, Drawing teacher, Hanamkonda for helping me by providing necessary drawings and charts.

Finally I thank my friend K. Ravindranath Gupta for his painstaking efforts in typing the dissertation.

P. SADANANDAM

1

Introduction

The caste system has developed in India as a rigid social structure since times immemorial. The controversy on the evolution of the *Varna* system of the Vedic age into *Jati* in the later period, still, continues to be debated in the academic circles. The existence of a complicated caste structure is visible in India atleast from the historical period as we find the reference of various occupational groups in Kautilya's *Arthasastra*. Despite the upward or downward social mobility in some cases, these occupational groups gradually evolved themselves into watertight compartments of rigid caste groups in respect of family relations like feasts, marriages and other specific rituals. In course of time, the original caste groups are divided into a number of sub-castes within the caste. Surprisingly a distinct nomadic tribe[1] has emerged as a minor sub-caste within each major artisan or professional caste under *Chaturvarnas* by the beginning of medieval period. The new sub-caste has certain duties to perform like keeping a record of the historical events or heroic deeds pertaining to the chiefs of their community and to serve as a cultural link between the generations by entertaining their community with the folklore. In all the artisan castes which have been the major production force in India, a sub-caste has come into being with a purpose to record the historical facts or the historic deeds of their ancestors as their heritage to be preserved for the coming generation in oral tradition and other theatrical forms. The present work is intended to study the oral history tradition and the art and culture of such marginalised nomadic tribes in Andhra Pradesh.

Objectives of Study

The objectives of the present study are :

(a) to evolve a methodological approach to the problems of oral history tradition

(b) to bring about native techniques of preserving the family histories of the house holds of a community and also to maintain the identity of the family and the community in the larger society.

(c) to find out the historicity of the facts articulated through oral narration and to trace the origin and history of the nomadic tribes as a sub-caste within the occupational communities.

Hypotheses

The study is intended to examine the following hypotheses in the light of the data collected.

(a) Indian caste system has survived many socio-religious reform movements which tried to demolish the rigid caste structure. But these movements had further added to the number of sub-castes and their divisions and sub-divisions.

(b) Each community or occupational castes could afford to maintain nomadic tribes to preserve their identity and heritage.

(c) The nomadic tribes came into being when a particular caste became a ruling class through upward social mobility, which could be observed atleast from the post-Mauryan times.

(d) Though the early phase of the history of these nomadic tribes is obscure, their presence has been effectively felt from the 10th and 11th centuries when the vernacular Telugu has gained the literary status.

Review of Literature

Preservation of historical information through oral tradition is being recognised as an authentic source of history in the recent times. Though we come accross very few studies on the theory and practice of oral tradition, significant progress is made in accepting the oral literature handed down to us through many generations in different art forms. In the light of the emerging attitude towards various forms of oral literature, a new awareness is created among the historians to reconsider the utility of the orally transmitted information which was hitherto rejected as myth. The fresh and live narrations of the professional singing groups are now being widely used in the reconstruction of our historical past.

A few studies are made in the West and the U.S. on the theory and practice of oral tradition. Charlotte-I, Lee has theorised in his book (*Oral Interpretation* U.S.A., 1959), that the past is lively enacted through the medium of oral interpretation. In India, the entertaining folks enliven the grandeur and the heroic acts of their illustrious predecessors for the benefit of the current generation. Another work by Jan Vansina (*Oral Tradition - A study in Historical Methodology*, London, 1965) makes significant contribution to introduce oral tradition as a historical method. The book analyses the oral tradition as an authentic mode of preservation of historical information from generation to generation. The work suggests certain precautions to be taken in collecting historical information from such oral records. James Hoopes in his book (*Oral History, an Introduction for Students*, North Corolina, 1980) develops an important theoretical link between the oral tradition and history. Allen Barbara, while acknowledging the importance of oral narration in re-constructing local history (*From Memory to History*, U.S.A., 1981), pointed out certain defficiencies of orally communicated hitstory such as its disregard for standard chronology ; clustering of oral acounts, telescoping historical time and dealing mostly with the family stories. Vladimir Propp wrote a seminal book,

(*Theory and History of Folklore,* U.S.A., 1984) highlighting the historicity of folklore. He feels that the events could also be dated exactly as they were caused by the actions of the people who really existed. Secondly, he recognises the folklore as the basis of history because the folklore deals with the "whole of a people's life throughout its existence".

The works of the foreign scholars as illustrated above were based on their experience and the data available to them locally. The generalisations, they made, are hypothetical conjectures which need critical examination in the context of the oral tradition in India. India, being a multilingual nation, offers a variety of forms of oral literature in each Indian language and also in the dialects of each major language. The different oral narrations are to be treated as *genres* with specific features of its own distinguishable from one another. Therefore, some scholars in Indian languages are attempting to record and study these oral forms which contribute to the explosure of their specific cultures.

In recent times some scholars in Telugu made considerable progress in the studies of oral literature and folk cultures. B. Rama Raju recorded many folk stories and oral literature in his pioneering work (*Telugu Janapada Geya Sahityam*, Hyderabad, 1958). He described the characteristic features of folk literature and also tried to trace their origin. Particularly he recorded the folk songs on women, children, working class etc. He made a reference to the cultural tradition of nomadic tribes within each major occupation caste.

P.S. Appa Rao published his thesis (*Telugu Nataka Vikasamu*, 1967) in which he described the origin and evolution of the Dance and Music of different Andhra Styles. He also brought to light the folk theatre like *Yakshaganas*, puppeteers etc. M. Radha Krishna Murthy contributed to the history of Theatre Art in Andhra (*Andhra Nataka Ranga Charitra*, Hyderabad, 1969) and focused light on folk dramatic forms. Thumati Dronappa described the folk art along with the profiles of folk artists in his work (*Janapada Kala Sampada*,

Hyderabad, 1972). B. Rama Raju and N. Krishna Kumari have jointly published a book (***Janapada Geyalu Sanghika Charitra***, Hyderabad, 1974) to emphasise that the oral literature is useful as an important source of social history. For the first time, they established the historical value of the Telugu folklore in general.

T.V. Subba Rao went a step further in codifying the oral narrations on a specific historical subject of Katamaraju and his times (*Katamaraju Kathalu*, Hyderabad, 1976). He threw light on the valuable historical information available from Katamaraju stories as preserved in the palm-leaf manuscripts. He made a reference to a number of controversial facts in the reconstruction of history of Katamaraju. G.S. Mohan highlighted the relevance of the folk literature with regard to the development of popular science and knowledge (*Janapada Vignana Vyasavali*, Ananthapur, 1981). R.V.S. Sundaram published a book on the singing groups of the entertaining sub-castes (*Janapada Sahityam*, Secunderabad, 1982). N Yadagiri Sharma made a systematic study on the entertaining folk in Andhra (Janapada Bikshuka Gayakulu, an unpublished Doctoral thesis, Osmania University, 1986). K. Mohan Rao also presented a significant work through his unpublished doctoral thesis on the 'History of Katamaraju and his times based on palm-leaf manuscripts'. Pulikonda Subba Chary made a systematic study on the literature of Nomadic tribes (Janapada Vignanam lo Asritha Sahityam, unpublished Doctoral thesis, Osmania University, Hyderabad, 1992).

These studies on Telugu folklore are explorative and serve as trend-setters. Most of these works are attempted by the specialists in Telugu language, literature and theatre arts from their points of view. Though they contributed to the historiography by illustrating the information on various historical events and personalities, these oral sources are yet to be treated scientifically. They have to be thoroughly examined and interpreted from the historical point of view. Therefore, the present work is an attempt to study the oral narratives of the nomadic tribes to trace the historicity of fading pastoral cultures as a result of intercultural conflicts during the early medieval period in Andhra which have now been marginalised in a different socio-economic set up in modern times.

Scope of Study

The distinct caste groups in the contemporary Indian society are not completely enumerated according to the statistics available from the Governmental sources. According to these statistics, the number of castes is around 366. In Andhra alone about 155 castes are listed. It is found that each caste has its own sub-caste which depends on that particular community for maintenance. Their origins are not yet traced so far. Most of them continued to stay atleast from the historical period. Even a broad survey of these sub-castes would become a voluminous work. Therefore, the present study is restricted to Vipravinodis, Bhatrajus, Viramustis, Pichikuntlas, Mandahechus, Runzas, Panasas, Kunapulis, Sadanasurulu, Patamus, Gangikutivaru, Goudajettis, Enutivaru, Pekkaras, Addam singas, Pandavulavaru, Kakipadigelavaru, Chindus, Dakkalis and Gurram malas who came into prominence by the beginning of medieval times. Their oral narratives both live and also those preserved in palm-leaf manuscripts are analysed in this study.

Organisation of Study

The study is presented in the following chapters :

Chapter one introduces the problem and explains the aims and objectives of the study. It proposes certain hypotheses to be tested in the present study. It reviews the important studies done earlier on this broad area of the subject and explains the methodology of the study.

Chapter two presents theoretical discussion on the orality and history. Various theories proposed by Western scholars are discussed to bringout the relevance of these studies to the Indian situation. The oral tradition as existed in India before the historical period and which still continues its existence among the entertaining folks is worthy of examination as a source of history. The merits and demerits of oral history are discussed in this chapter to highlight the historiographical significance of the oral literary forms.

Chapter three attempts to trace the evolution of the caste system and its development as a complicated socio-economic structure. The division and the sub-divisions of these castes have led to the origin of the nomadic tribes who sing the glory of their ancestors through theatrical performances are described and their role in the preservation of family histories is discussed from the historical perspective.

Chapter four describes the life and culture of nomadic tribes who give their performances with the help of illustrations maps and other exhibits.

Chapter five gives a critical analysis of various source material available on the heroic acts of their ancestors among the patron-community. The stories often retold by the nomadic tribes are analysed and recorded during the field work and compared with the palm-leaf manuscripts which are retained with the singing troupes. Besides manuscripts, the other sources like Kaifiyats and inscriptions were also critically assesssed in order to bring out the historicity of these oral narrations.

Chapter six presents the findings of this study which help historicity of various events which form part of the subject matter of the oral narrations of these tribes.

Methodology

The present work is based on the Historical Method broadly, but the Observation and Empirical Methods are also employed since the study required field work. The 'Open-ended' interviews were conducted with the nomadic tribes to record the historical data preserved through oral tradition and also to elicit information regarding their customs, traditions and rituals. District Gazetteers, Manual reports and Kaifiyats were consulted in the A.P. State Archives, Hyderabad. The works of the Western scholars on orality and oral history were consulted in the library of A.S.R.C.* Hyderabad. Various books and journals on folklore traditions, both in English and Telugu are consulted from the libraries of Osmania University,

* American Studies Research Centre.

Potti Sriramulu Telugu University, University of Hyderabad, State Central Library and Srikrishnadevarayandhrabhasha Nilayam etc. The epigraphical sources were collected from the library of State Department of Archaeology, Hyderabad. Besides books, number of articles published on folklore and nomadic tribes and their narrations which appeared in the periodicals like Bharathi, and special numbers of Andhra Patrika are collected from State Central Library, Hyderabad.

Besides the written sources both secondary and primary, the researcher conducted field work and located some singing nomadic groups in some places of Andhra Pradesh. He collected the copies of the palm-leaf manuscripts and photographed their artistic possessions like the terracotta images and other theatrical material. He had also recorded their oral narrations on audio tapes. He conducted open ended interviews with many of the active performers of different age groups ranging from thirty to sixty five years. Their responses were compiled and compared with the literary sources to prove the authenticity of the oral information.

Limitations of Study

The study is partly based on the participatory observation method to record the oral narratives of mobile nomadic troupes attached to various castes. The transliterations of audio tapes suffer certain defects in audition and understanding. The absence of corraborative evidence in writing further complicates the problems. The palm-leaf manuscripts and copper plates are only copies of the obscure originals telescoping in time. Since the stories are related to the unlettered communities, the historicity of such events is found difficult to be established satisfying all the norms of authenticity. However, the events of oral tradition would enable us to record the details regarding the culture, life and historical events of that period.

Relevance of the Study

The study is significant because it helps understand the traditional forms of preservation of family and community history. However, though painstaking, it is a rewarding experience to record and preserve the oral literature for the posterity. It studies the origin and evolution of various sub-castes and nomadic tribes within a community so that the contemporary social stratification in India could be understood in a proper perspective.

Reference

1. On account of their dependence on the professional or artisan caste for their livelihood they are referred in the modern Telugu literature as *kulabikshaka gayakulu* (కుల భిక్షక గాయకులు) and the term is translated into English as "Begging sub-caste" or parasitic sub-caste. As a matter of fact, they are not beggers in common parlance. They are nomadic tribes within a major caste. The caste house-holds are expected to support them to keep alive their tradition, custom, family and tribe's history and folk art forms. Therefore, such sub-castes are termed as marginalised nomadic tribes in this dissertation. Secondly, what they receive from their patrons should not be considered as 'alms' in its ordinary meaning but it is a compensation provided by the community for their service. So we treat this compensation as a commitment or a donation.

2

Oral History Tradition

Man has an innate urge to know and to transmit his knowledge and under standing to others. The pre-literate people had developed their own methods of enquiry based on observation and evolved certain forms of expression through art and oral presentation. The most striking phenomenon of the pre-literate oral forms was the standardized textual form[1] which could not be eroded or interpolated in course of time. Their forms of expression were designed in a rigid frame. Secondly, each work has a peculiar style and rhythm which is unique. Thus, any interpolations or omissions or commissions could be traced out by a serious scholar.

An attempt is made in this chapter to give a broad outline of the recent studies on the oral history tradition in the West and to compare and contrast the same with the oral tradition and folk art forms in Indian vernaculars.

Well-structured languages were already developed long before the script appeared on seals, earthen tablets, barch skin, stone, copper plates, leaves, cloth etc., All these writing material suffer from certain inadequacies. Long narratives could not be recorded on these material. Except for the stone and metal plates, the others are perishable. Secondly, as a caution the ancient scholars did not reduce them to writing because there is a danger that these writings might fall in the hands of those who may misuse them. Thirdly, they preferred oral transmission of the knowledge from teacher to the taught directly. Last but not the least, a written document is susceptible to alterations and interpolations. Therefore, the ancient people preferred the oral transmission of knowledge from one generation to the other for which they depended more on unfailing collective memory for preservation of knowledge.

Orality was associated with the strong bond to tradition[2] to prevent its flexibility. These traditions played a very important role in the pre-literate societies. Tradition ensures continuity which is the primary requisite of oral transmission. As conventions are more strictly followed than a written law, the tradition maintains the oral structures surviving through innumerable generations. Each generation inherits many elements of social life, like customs, institutions, speech, dress, laws, songs and tales from the preceding generation and acquires a few novelties or adopts some elements from other contemporary societies. However each society is judged by its transmitted elements of social life for its value[3]. When an old or long established idea is still accepted by a considerable section of a community, the tradition acquires social significance. As the traditions with which we are concerned are myths, we should take into account the salient features of myth. A myth is a narrative of events; the narrative has a sacred quality the sacred communication is made in symbolic form; at least some of the events and objects which occur in the miyth neither occur nor exist in the world other than that of the myth itself ; and the narrative refers in dramatic form to origins or transformations, what is more, a myth is like a palimpsest on which generation after generation has engraved its own layer of massages and we must decipher each layer with a different code book[4]. The primary characteristics of tradition are identified as vagueness, remoteness of sources and wide ramification with which it seems "peculiarly strong to those who have recourse to it and peculiarly weak to those who mean to reject it[5].

History is viewed, interpreted and recorded in different ways by different generations. Defferent forms of narration were designed and followed depending on the social, cultural and political situations. Thus, a number of forms of narration have survived through the ages in the oral tradition of history[6]. All the primordial societies were bound by tradition which preserved their identities and peculiarities in their characters. Even after some such societies turned civilized, they still continued the oral tradition to keep their collective memory fresh through the innumerable generations.

Despite the inevitability of mortality, man longs for permanence and living beyond. To overcome the physical disability to live forever, man tries to live through his work of art or literature. Whatever he chooses to be remembered by his progeny, he attempts to preserve the information through a select form of art. Thus all the literary traditions of the earlier generations in any form are the expressions of their feelings and experiences which conform to the basic tenents of Historiography.

The form and method of History however change from time to time responding to the emerging needs, aspirations and demands. History is rewritten by each generation in a peculiar form of its own by drawing the content from the earlier natives. Thus, all earlier forms of narration become source material for the historians of the succeeding generations[7]. By the advent of modern times, literacy was restricted to a small section of people due to historic compulsions. Moreover, the writing as such was limited to the documentation of very important grants by the members of royal family or chieftains or wealthy merchants. Therefore, history in general had to be preserved through oral tradition till very recent times.

The different forms of oral tradition may be categorised as narratives, legends, anecdotes, proverbs and historical lays. Further in the narratives based on first-hand eyewitness reports may distinguish from those based on second-hand or hearsay reports of events which have become legends[8]. In European societies, the oral tradition is limited to the exchanges that take place in the course of everyday conversation in a random fashion as anecdotes. In other societies (Non-European) where pre literate tribes of people still exist, rich oral tradition of different forms are found. "Long before the appearance of professional historians, amateurs living among pre-literate peoples collected oral traditions, and although not in the least interested in the theoretical aspect of the question, used them to reconstruct the past of these peoples. It may be said that the first historical writings based on oral traditions all date from the time when the first European explorers arrived upon the scene, and very nearly all that we know today about the early history of these pre-literate peoples is due to such amateur historians"[9].

Of all the forms, tales are generally less trustworthy than other types of soruce. But in contrast to formulae, poetry, lists and commentaries, they are the only sources which give a detailed account of a series of events. They alone exhibit a historical perspective. The various types of tales are of very unequal value, simply because they are so different. Historical tales are mainly useful as sources of information about military, political, social, institutional and legal history. Didactic tales provide information about cultural values. Artistic tales have, on the whole, little value except for the history of psychological attitudes, whereas tales containing personal recollections can be used as sources of information for all forms of history[10].

All historical tales are official traditions aimed at recording history. They are recited by specialists on ceremonial occasions, and are transmitted within a particular social group. Three types can be distinguished; those concerning general history, local history and family history[11].

They are always official traditions, and thus extremely prone to distortion in defence of public interests. But they give a general survey of the past history of the people concerned, and show the main lines of development[12].

They differ from the foregoing not only because they recount the past of small local units within a state, but also because they donot, as a rule, go very far back into the past, and they are transmitted with much less care, for there are no proper specialists for this purpose and their recital is not subjected to the same strict control as the tales concerning general history. They usually narrate the history of a family, a clan, or a village[13].

They deal with the past history of lineages. In many societies which have no centralised forms of government, they replace general histories. Very often their family tales are mere outgrowths of genealogies. They explain why two branches of a family have seperated and no longer live together. Tales of this kind contain many stereotype phrases. Family traditions do not, however, disappear in societies with State organization. They may even become the general history of the society, either because the family history in question is that of the dynasty, or because the general history consists of a number of family histories. In addition to dynastic traditions, most of the important families whose members hold official positions preserve a knowledge of their family history. It is noticeable that such family histories all tend to follow the same lines being designed to vindicate the family's privileged position and establish some sort of a link with the ruling house[14].

The folklore or legends which are verbal stories passed on from one generation to the next. Every art including folklore is derived from reality and reflects it[15] Oral history is based on spoken documents such as songs, speeches interviews etc., which are very useful for history. The folklore legend and song are preserved by memory and later transmitted orally to the next generation. In illiterate societies the professional story tellers are found whose job is to learn the story of the past from elders and then pass it on to the next generation.

One major difficulty in the verbal art is that the common people are transformed into grand heroes accomplishing the greatest exploits which can only be sung by others. To trace the historicity from the folklore becomes difficult as the realities are transformed into quasi-history with change of time[16]. But historical legends treat events and persons of the past as if they were real. By preserving the memory of past events and narrating about the heroic behaviour of some person, the historical legend lives in the people's memory as oral history[17]

The advantages of the oral tradition over the literary tradition are manyfold. In the oral tradition the content and the form are standardized in a rigid frame that events are dramatised for each succeeding generation without any interpolations. In Indian oral tradition in contrast to its European counterpart we will find a sub-caste within a caste who enact the past events of their interest as their only occupation.

The oral tradition adds "feelings" to the events unlike the dry literary narrations. Because of this peculiar character, the people would patronise this sub-caste by encouraging periodical performances so that the oral tradition has a continuum.

The oral tradition speaks general history of common man to a large extent since the literature is the product of a very small section of the literate elite which emerged in the historical period. The subject matter of the literary forms is generally drawn from the ruling class or elite society. Thus the oral tradition takes care of the aspirations of the majority.

In the light of the modern historical method, which is approximately two centruries old, oral tradition is discounted on the grounds of doubtful authenticity. The doubts are generally raised on the reliability of memory carried through a number of generations[18]. The historicity of European oral traditions have suffered a great deal, because, the European societies have turned out to be complete literate communities since atleast a couple of centuries by now. The written word has gained sanctity and precedence over the spoken word.

But Indian society has a rich oral tradition in the standardized oral texts of the Vedas from times immemorial. Lot of care is taken by Indians in preserving the original texts intact through generations within a rigid poetic and musical frame work. The wrong spelling and mispronunciation are treated as great sins and believed that even a small error in the presentation invites a curse. Therefore, the oldest oral texts are still read in the same style and connotation in all parts of India despite the development of different vernaculars. This has facilitated the Europeans to record the ancient texts and translate them into European languages while the Western classics are considered eternal by them because they are forever fixed and frozen as written documents. They had a misconception that the Indian traditions are fluid and mythified. On the other hand the Indian texts are preserved orally intact for atleast 3,000 years from now. Therefore, "the relationship between orality and fluidity in these texts is the reverse of what one might expect if one simply extrapolated from what we think we know of Western Classics"[19].

The kind of information that the oral sources provide differs quite often from that which contained in written records. The fact is that the great deal of what people remember about the past had simply gone unrecorded. The difference between the oral and the written sources arises from the very nature of medium of communication they adopt. The general criticism on the oral sources pertains to its characteristics. These characteristics include "disregard for standard chronology; emotional association of persons as a primary organizing principle ; clustering of oral accounts around significant events or persons ; reliance on visual imagery and striking detail ; compression or telescoping of historical times ; displacement of original actors in a historical event with others; migration of dramatic narrative elements among historical accounts ; and patterning of oral accounts of different events along similar lines"[20].

By and large in the Indian oral tradition, the chronology and the details of the events are well preserved in different forms of the narrations in case of the events occurred atleast from the early medieval period onwards. However the attempts of these forms to link the events with the distant past for the purpose of continuity invite criticism on their authenticity. The oral accounts of this period can also be corroborated with the written records to a large extent. These written records may sometimes differ with the oral accounts on aspects of chronology. But we have scores of epigraphical evidence where two epigraphs on the same subject differ with each other on many aspects. While the written records facilitated preserving the history of the ruling and the wealthy class, the history of common people of tribes and local history are mostly recorded in the oral tradition. Thus, valuable information is preserved in the oral form.

The tradition of oral communication of history of the past also includes oral interpretation[21] by the performer of a particular art from designed for the purpose. Through oral interpretation the authors intent is communicated to the audience by oral recreation of literature with a purpose to evoke the desired response from the audience. The performer gives the whole credit of the work to the author and declares himself as a middle man or instrument of communication.

Thus, orally communicative history creates a number of images and details of the events stamping vivid pictures of the past in the minds of listener[22]. Similarly traditional family histories focus "on pioneer experiences....... how the family fortune was made or lost : or the family's involvement in wars, economic depressions and other trauma inducing occurrences"[23].

Sumup

Oral narratives are now being recognised as valuable sources of history in the absence of an authentic written record. These narratives are of immense value particularly in connection with the historical writings on the culture and life of the un-lettered mass. Though it is a hypothetical conjecture the written and the archaeological sources mostly reflect the life of dominant class in the society. The references to common man in these sources appear to be mere coincidences.

In continents like Europe, America and Australia, most of the aboriginal tribes are depleting in their number at a faster rate under the pressure of modern civilisation. The societies in Asia and Africa are also shedding their pastoral and agrarian cloak giving place to modernity. The modern historiography in India came into existence during the colonial phase. The colonial historiography with its two paradoxical shades of opinions - administrative and nationalistic - has mostly depended on the convetional sources of history, namely archaeological and literary. The oral tradition of preserving the past in India dates back to the times immemorial. These narratives were ignored hitherto as legendary myths. Most of the ancient literature which has been handed down from generation to generation through oral tradition is judged ahistorical. Besides Sanskrit literature, we come across numerous narratives through oral art forms which are still currently practised among various communities and castes in India. These sources if tapped, analysed, and interpreted with scientific temper will provide rich information on the history and culture of bygone days. The study of such narratives also reveal the historic sense of the unlettered communities to fossilise their cultures and maintain their identities braving the vagaries of time.

India is a pluralistic society with different religions and castes. Caste system is peculiar to India though other peoples are also socially stratified. Each caste tried to preserve its identity by mainitaining their own entertaining folks who sing the glory of their great ancestors. These oral narratives are yet to be explored, analysed and studied to understand the subaltern cultures in India. These narrations or unconventional sources may also facilitate the reconstruction of history and culture of the people.

References

1. The artificial standards of correct speech were developed in certain language groups with the primary concern for the maintenance of a standard pronunciation and diction.

   Edwin R.A. Seligman (ed), **Encyclopaedia of the Social Science**, Vol. 15, Newyork, 1935, p. 64.

2. Tradition is derived from the word 'tradere' which generally means to transmit. Thus tradition is that which has been handed down, if

not through all generations, atleast through more than one. Edwin R.A. Seligman (ed), *op.cit.,* p. 63.

3. *Ibid*, p. 62.
4. Murthy, M.L.K., Social and Economic History as reflected in folk traditions and myths in Andhra Pradesh, **A.P. History Congress proceedings**, Vol. IX, Anakapalle, 1988, pp. 5-16.
5. Edwin R.A. Seligman (ed) : *op. cit.,* p. 67.
6. "These communicative mechanisms interact in complex ways". Edwin R.A. Seligman : *op.cit.,* p. 90.
7. The pioneering work of Bernheim, A Feder and Baner contributed much to the research studies on oral tradition and its value as historical source material.
8. Bernheim.E, Einletiung in der Geschichtswissenschaft as quoted from Janvansina, **Oral Tradition a study in Historical Methodology**, London, 1965, p. 3.
9. Janvansina, *op.cit.,* p. 7.
10. Janvansina, *op.cit.,* p. 154.
11. Ibid, p. 155.
12. Ibid, p. 155.
13. Ibid, p. 156.
14. Janvansina, *op.cit.,* p. 156.
15. Vladimir Propp. **Theory and History of Folklore**, Manchester University Press, 1984, p. 48.
16. Ramaraju, B. **Telugu Janapada Geya Sahityam** (Telugu), Hyderabad, 1978, p. 178.
17. Cicero, V.I. as quoted in Vladimir Propp, *op.cit.,* p. 51.
18. "The argument that the human memory cannot be trusted has been disproved by research among groups of people around the world who have a marked propensity for retaining historical truths over long periods of time. Ethnohistorians have demonstrated the veracity of orally communicated history among American, Indian, African and South Asian groups whose cultures - are overwhelmingly oral and rich in ancient historical traditions. Studies in these areas indicated that, while orally communicated

history thrives best in a non-literate culture, it is preserved with considerable accuracy under certain favourable social and cultural conditions".

Barbara Allan, **From Memory to History : Using Oral Sources in local Historical Research**. American Association for state and local History, 1981, p. 69.

19. Wendy Doniger O'Flaherty, "Impermanance and Eternity in Indian Art and Myth" in Carle M. Borden (ed), **Contemporary India**, Delhi, 1989, p. 79.
20. Barbara, Allen *op. cit.*, p. 26.
21. "Oral interpretation is sometimes referred to as oral reading, reading aloud, reading to others, interpretative reading, interpretative speech" Charlotte, I, Lee, **Oral interpretation,** 2nd edition, Cambridge, 1959, p. 3.
22. Barbara, Allen , *op.cit.,* p. 33
23. *Ibid*, pp. 39, 40.

3

Art and Culture of Theatrical Performers

Society is a system in which people live together in organised communities. There has been a continual change for the past 6000 years in the *Chaturvarna* system of the Indian society, which in course of time led to the formation of several castes and creeds. The people belonging to different castes pursued different occupations in accordance with their caste to earn their livelihood. There is no coherent relation between the Vedic society and that of the present. There is a radical change in the society between the past and the present. The political system had undergone a sea change and along with it the life styles of people and their professions had undergone a change beyond any recognition causing social mobility within the structure of the society.

The internal mobility in the caste structures which came about in the wake of Saiva, Vaishnava and Shakthi movements led to the creation of a unique mendicant class in the society. These, inturn, became exponents of arts and folk literature. These entertaining folks who are on the wane now, propagated the caste histories and received alms in return. The present chapter attempts to analyse the legendary accounts connected with the origin of some major castes and respective nomadic tribes. The upper castes namely Brahmins, Kshatriyas and Vaisyas have only one nomadic tribe each for their exclusive entertainment. But the Sudras being a social category include numerous castes each with one or more than one nomadic tribes[1].

While the *Chaturvarna* system originated in the Vedic society, several occupational castes emerged in course of time and categorised under the *Sudra* community. From the beginning of the historical period, several such communities rose to prominence and also new kingdoms emerged under the powerful *Sudra* dynasties by the medieval period. During the Kakatiya rule, the *Basavapuranam* of Palkurki Somana and *Paramayogi Vilasamu* of Thiruvengalanathudu contributed to the widespread popularity of the Veera Saiva and Veera Vaishnava religious movements respectively. In course of time, people belonging to these religions were split into many more new castes like Balizas, Jangas, Thamballu, Bhavanis in Saivite religion and Nambas, Sathanis, Dasaries, Devadasis in Vaishnavite religion[2]. There was considerable impact of Basaveshwara on Saivism and Ramanuja on Vaishnavism. These religions influenced a great deal the fine arts like painting, sculpture, dance and music.

The nomadic tribes enjoyed much importance as well as respect during the rule of Reddys, Velamas and Vijayanagara dynasties[3]. During this period the religious preachers of Saiva and Vaishnava cults were also honoured. Hence they were able to propagate the aims and objectives of their cults among the people. They further paved a way for the creation of mendicant class in each caste.

About the origin of such singing groups, B. Rama Raju opines[4] that rulers employed certain singing groups to provide entertainment in their military camps during the wars and also to encourage the soldiers to fight on the lines of their illustrious predecessors. After the war was over, these singing groups were attached to each producing caste for their maintenance during the peace times. Therefore, these singing groups collected information about the castes on which they depended so as to please their hosts for liberal grants. In course of time, these folks formed part of these castes and remained dependant on them perennially.

The nomadic tribes recite caste myths, legends and historical events of their patron-communities developing their own styles, methods and forms of art. Some of them recite the stories on open dais while the others exhibit wall hangings called *Patams* for their narrations. Therefore, the nomadic tribes may be classified as *Patapradarshana Kathakulu* and theatrical art performers. In the art of *Patapradarshana Katha* they exhibit *Patam* in which the entire caste *Puranas* of their patron-community are printed in the form of pictures. In the theatrical art form the members of the troupe make-up themselves according to the needs of their characters in the story to recite to their patrons and perform on the open air stage. This chapter deals with the art and culture of those nomadic tribes who perform on the stages erected temporarily for the performance.

Brahman Community

Vipravinodis

This class of mendicants take donations from Brahmins only[5]. They are Lingayats known as Vipravinodis because they perform acrobatic feats to entertain the *Vipras* or Brahmins. The word *Vipra* means a Brahmin and *Vinodi* means an entertainer with their magical tricks. In a note on the Vipravinodis, C. Hayavadana Rao writes that they are said to be the descendants of a Brahmin and Lingayat woman[6]. Gurubrahmasharma mentioned a legend about the Vipravinodis in his work *Kondaveeti Samrajyam*. There is also another legend[7] as mentioned in Vidyaranya's Shankara Vijayamu, which explains why they depend on Brahmins alone. They generally go from place to place with their families.

One of their favorite feats is throwing up three stones or wooden balls in the air and catching them or rolling them over various parts of body. When they perform this play before a mixed audience, they call themselves *Naravidyavaru*, which is said to be an abbreviated form of *narulu meche vidyalu chese varu* or those who perform praise worthy feats[8].

Historically this magic was very popular between 15th and 17th centuries. These Vipravinodis were adoring the Vijayanagara court[9]. Accordig to the inscription of Sadasivarayalu[10], the Vipravinodis were in large number in Vijayanagara kingdom and they also held *Agraharas.*

Their magic is called *Vipravinodi vidya*. They are a sub-sect in Brahmin caste. Moreover, they have various *Gotras* and *Sutras*. They also give donations for divine purposes. They pray God and perform magic with charms. Vipravinodis were performing their magic in the courts and palaces of the kings and also in the households of Brahmins[11].

The magic show of the Vipravinodis lasts for half an hour or less than one hour. Their magic instruments consist of 4 or 5 bamboo sticks, 2 or 3 shawls, two palm-leaf books, one common drum, one Harmonium, and other such instruments. At the time of the magic show, they plant 4 bamboo sticks in four corners and cover it with shawls like curtains. They put an empty almirah behind the curtains. Some members of the troupe start the *Bhajan* marking the beginning of the show. Later, they raise the curtains to show the empty almirah to audience as shown in fig.1. Then the leader of the troupe goes behind the curtains with palm-leaf books and stays there for some time. Meantime the *Bhajan* goes on when they raise the curtain again. The almirah is seen with full of idols of gods, lamps, flowers, and offerings as shown in fig.2. After the end of the show they go to the Brahmin houses and attract them with their magic by creating idols, stones, snakes, scorpions and sacred ash etc.

There is one more important magic event 'Rope trick' which the Vipravinodis perform. It was performed even during the days of the British rule in Andhra. These details are recorded and appreciated by many foreign magicians like Paul Daniel of England. Many foreign news papers also wrote about this magic trick in those days[12].

The Rope trick is performed in the following manner. Two brothers of Vipravinodi team perform this event by showing a rope to the audience and asking them to examine it, who gather in an open field to witness the event. After their examination the elder one throw the rope up into the sky which appears to the audience as a stiff stick. Later, the younger one climbs up into the sky on the stick and disappears. Then the rope falls on the ground and the elder one shouts loudly and asks the audience where his brother has gone. After two minutes, the younger one would comes and joins the audience from behind the crowd, making all the onlookers spell bound.

Vipravinodis were very popular during Vijayanagara period. They used to entertain the public with their open stage performances of various tricks and magics. After the decline of the native kingdoms, they had to depend on general public and slowly the art has faded away. Now we can hardly find them giving any performances. It is also said that the present way of life does not permit the continuance of such art performances any more. A trace of their existence could still be found in the parts of Nellore district and Rayalaseema.

Kshatriya Community

Bhatrajus

The Bhatrajus are also called Bhatmurtis, Bhatwandlu and Bhats. The Bhatrajus lived in kings' courts to flatter them and to sing glory of their ancestors[13].

Regarding the origin of the Bhatrajus, a legend says that King Prataparudra (1295-1323) of Warangal had induced some Brahmins with huge amounts of money to conduct religious ceremonies in the houses of his Velama chiefs whose exact caste was not known as they came from north and took refuge in his court. Such Brahmins were ex-communicated by the Brahmin community. They were forced to accept matrimonial relations from lower castes like Velamas and Kapus. Thus, a new mixed caste has emerged. This new caste was patronized by Velamas and Kapus. The Bhatrajus depended on them for their livelihood[14].

There is another legend that King Prataparudra had invited the Bhats (Bhatrajus in Telugu) from north India and employed them in his court as jests for entertainment. After the fall of Kakatiya kingdom, they lived in the courts of Reddy and Velama chiefs praising their valour. But most of these Bhatrajus were well-versed in Telugu language and literature. The most illustrious of them was Ramarajabhushana of the Vijayanagara court who wrote the famous work *Vasucharitra*[15].

Yet another legend is recorded by E. Thurston that one Pillalamarri Bethala Reddy had three sons of whom two sons took up agriculture and the third joined military service under the Kakatiyas. The third one got 74 sons who were also recruited in the army. Their lives were saved by a clever Bhatraju from the wrath of King Prataparudra who wanted to punish them for their indiscipline. As a gratitude, these Reddy chiefs started patronising the Bhatrajus[16].

The Bhatrajus not only praised the rajas but also encouraged their soldiers in the battle fields through heroic songs. They also served as mediators between different kings. Besides these, they used to follow the army to the battle fields to encourage and entertain the soldiers during nights. After returning from the battle field, these Bhatrajus composed songs orally describing the valour of their king and the heroic fight of the army. Thus, the people came to know the details of war through them[17].

These Bhatrajus wear the sacred thread across their shoulders like the Brahmins and they are well-versed in the traditional literature. They sing from the great epics, the *Ramayana* and the *Mahabharata* besides the heroic deeds of ancient Kshatriya rulers. They call themselves, Rajus, claiming half descent from the ancient Kshatriya clans as the offsprings of Kshatriya female by the Vaisya male.

After the fall of the Kakatiyas, some of them also went to the courts of the Vijayanagara and the Bahamanis. They received patronage both from the Hindu and the Muslim rulers[18].

They keep oral records of the ancient family histories and the genealogies of the ruling class, the Velama and Kapu communities. They participate in all the important occasions in Velama and Kapu households. They flatter the head and other members of these families and receive gifts.

The Bhatrajus are Vaishnavites, worshipping Vishnu in the form of Venkateshwara, and following the guidance of Sri Vaishnava Brahmins in religious matters. Every member of the caste is required to be initiated with the *Ashtakshari Mantra* (eight-syllabled mantra) of Vishnu, and marked with *Mudras* (*sankha*-conch and *chakra*-wheel) on his arms. Females worship goddess Gouri during the Dipavali festival. The favourite deity of children is Lord Ganesh, who presides over arts and learning. Members of the caste have a strong belief in magic and ghosts; malignant deities, such as Maisamma and Pochamma who are appeased on Sundays by sacrificing fowls. Brahmins are employed on ceremonial and religious occasions.

Marriage outside the caste is prohibited. A man may marry two sisters, but two brothers cannot marry two sisters. Marriage with the daughter of a sister is allowed. A man cannot marry any of his first cousins, except the daughter of his maternal uncle or paternal aunt[19].

Bhatraju girls are married either as infants or as adults. It is not customary to offer girls to temples or trees. A girl committing adultery is ex-communicated. A second wife is only taken in case the first wife is barren or incurably diseased. The marriage ceremony does not differ materially from the komatis. A Brahmin is consulted in fixing an auspicious date for the wedding. *Kanyadanam* and *Pusthe*, *Mattelu* form the essential portions of the ceremony. The bridegroom, at the time of the *Polu* is presented with *Gantam* (an iron pan) and a book of palm leaves, which symbolises the hereditary occupation of the caste. Widows are not allowed to marry again, nor is divorce recognised. An adulterous wife is expelled from the caste. In matters of inheritance the caste is guided by the Hindu law. In the absence of male issue, females are entitled to inherit.

The social status of the Bhatrajus rank below Kapus and Velamas. They eat food from the hands of Brahmins, Komatis, Ayyawarus, Velamas, Sathanis and Gollas. The Kuruma, Telaga, Rajaka, and Mutrasis eat from their hands. They are non-vegetarians and drink liquor. Now many of them have taken to cultivation and hold lands on various tenures. Some of them have entered Government service. Some hold ***Inam*** lands (rent free) which are mostly grants of an ancient date. We find them largely in entire Telugu speaking areas of Andhra Pradesh.

Komati Community (Vaisyas)

Viramustis

The Viramustis are attached to the Vaisyas for their maintenance. They are very well known among all the nomadic tribes. They are also called Virabhatas or Bhadrapadas. The word 'Viramusti' is derived from Sanskrit *Vira* means warrior and *Musti* means fist. These mendicants are Veera Saivas. They also take donations from Lingayats, Balijas and Jangamas. But the Vaisyas are the chief patrons of the Viramustis, because they sing about Goddess *Kanyaka* the main deity of the Vaisyas. A hand bell and a conch are the musical instruments of Viramustis (Fig-1, 2). They sing in praise of the Lord Siva, waving a long sword. Viramustis are mentioned in the Telugu literary works[20] and inscriptions[21] from 10th and 11th centuries onwards when Saivism became a prominent religion through its militant sect of Veera Saivism.

There are several legends regarding the origin of Viramustis. Of these, two are very popular. One of them traces their origin from the sweat of Veerabhadra who destroyed the *Daksha Yagna*[22], and other connects them to the episode of King Vishnuvardhana who wanted to marry a Vaisya girl later came to be worshipped as Goddess Kanyaka by the Vaisya community[23].

In recognition of the services of Viramustis the Vaisyas promised to maintain them forever. The Viramustis also take donations from the Jangamas and Saivas on the plea that they assisted Virabhadra in destroying the *Daksha Yagna*. But mostly they depend on the Vaisya community and keep the oral records of the family histories of the Vaisyas and sing ballads in praise of their chief deity, Vasavi Kanyaka. They also assist the Vaisya households in important rituals. On certain festival days the Viramustis worship Lord Siva by taking part in the religious processions. On these occasions they perform ritual dances uttering certain words to the accompaniment of musical instruments such as hand bells, conches etc. Further on Sivaratri day and during the auspicious months of *Sravana* and *Kartika* the Viramustis worship Lord Siva in *Sivakshetras* with colourful religious processions by taking out *Prabhas*[24]. The Viramustis deem it their right to carry these *Prabhas* in procession to the famous Siva temples such as Srisailam and Kotappakonda. Sometimes the *Prabhas* bigger in size are carried on bullock-carts. On these occasions the idols of Lord Virabhadra and Goddess Kanyaka made of either copper or bronze are beautifully decorated with floral garlands and taken out in procession with the *Prabhas* (Fig. 3 & 4).

The Viramustis express their devotional fervour in many queer and grotesque ways. One of them is *Narasa*. In this the devotee impales his tongue and sometimes his throat with large sized needles and does ritual dance (Fig. 5, 6 & 7). *Narasa* is a derivative of *Naracha* which means an arrow used for impaling. There are different kinds of *Narasas*. If the throat is impaled it is called 'Throat narasa' likewise they have eye *Narasa* in which eyelids are pierced. The devotion of the Viramustis is marked by heightened emotional fervour.

Such frightening scenes of devotion are more often seen at *Kshetras* like Srisailam, Chintapalli, Korivi, Chintalapudi, Amalapuram, Draksharamam, Vemulawada, Kaleshwaram, and Kothakonda. While some frenzied devotees pierce their tongues with needles, a few others burn camphor either on their tongue or palm. Such practices make Viramustis prominent among the communities of the entertaining folks.

The Viramustis believe their original occupation to be taking donations from Komatis and they sell balls of *Vibhuti* (holy ash). They extort donations by beating themselves, scratching their bodies with sword and pricking themselves with needles. They carry, a sword, a needle an image of Virabhadra and the head of Daksha as a badge of their mendicancy. At a komati marriage they claim one rupee from the boy's party and eight *annas* (half a rupee) from the girl's party as their perquisites. Their women are skilful tatooers and make mats of leaves of the wild date. After initiation into this order, the Viramusti men are enjoined not to cut the hair of their heads or beards[25].

Generally Viramustis go about for taking donations before Dasara festival, because the Vaisyas close the annual accounts of their trade and open new accounts from Dasara festival. Most of the Vaisyas worship goddess Kanyaka during the festival in which Viramustis definitely take part. So the Viramustis prepare to visit Vaisya houses during Dasara festival. Every Viramusti family has jurisdiction over some villages for taking donations. These villages called *Mirasi* Villages of that particular Viramusti family. They only beg from their *Mirasi* villages and they do not venture to trespass into others' villages. If they do so, that would be considered as crime and they would be awarded punishments in *Kula Panchayats* and penalty would be imposed on them.

The traditional *Mirasi* rights over a village are transferable to the sons of the family. In case of the absence of male child the rights can be given to sons-in-law. If no child is there (male or female) the same rights can be sold out to some others according to the wishes of the family head. These rights can be also leased out for one or two years to any one for some amount fixed in an agreement between them or can be sold out permanently.

The Viramustis visit Penukonda every year on Sivaratri day to participate in the celebrations of Kanyaka festival, which takes place every year. They get a certificate in Penukonda after participating in the festival from *Vaisya Kula Peetam*, situated there. In all the certificates given by *Kula peetam* to them, inscribed about the permission to take donations from Vaisyas. It is a renewal certificate. They show this certificate to Vaisyas when they visit them. In some places particularly at Piduguralllu, and Macherla there is a register with the head of Vaisya caste. He enters the names of Viramustis to stop the repetition of them.

The Viramustis visit the Vaisya houses once in six months, because they have two types of *Mirasi* villages i.e. *Sthala* and

Parasthala[26]. This type of *Mirasis* is not found in other nomadic tribes. But these two *Mirasis* are not held by one family. The different Viramusti families take donations from these *Sthala* and *Parasthala Mirasi* villages.

The social rank of this caste is very low and none except the lowest uncleaned classes will take food from them. It is said that they accept cooked food only from Komatis and Balijas. They are Saivites. They follow Saiva customs in their day to day life. They are all *Vibhutidharis* and acknowledge *Aradhya* Brahmins as their *Gurus*. Some of them are converted to *Lingayatism* and wear the lingam on their arms. Their chief god is Virabhadra, who is worshipped by them on every Monday and on Sivaratri day with a variety of offerings. A fast is also observed in honour of the God. In addition to this the members of the caste revere Pochamma Mutyalamma, and other village deities.

Viramustis marry their daughters off before they have attained the age of puberty, but adult marriages occasionally take place if the girl's parents are too poor to arrange her marriage before puberty. Pre-marital sex is not tolerated, and in such a case if the man is from her own caste, he is compelled to pay a fine to the caste people and take her as his wife. If he is already married, and declines to fulfill his obligations towards her, he is required to maintain her until she finds some one in the caste who would marry her by the rite of *Marumanuvu*. Polygamy is permitted in principle to some extent[27].

After the preliminary negotiations have been concluded, and the horoscopes of the couple have been found to tally, an auspicious day is fixed for the celebration of the wedding. A marriage pandal of six pillars is eracted infront of the bride's house and another at the bridegroom's house. The ceremonies of *Prathanam Eadurukollu katna* and *Ironi* follow and need no separate description, as they closely correspond with those of the other Telugu castes. In the *Mylapolu* the pair is bathed and seated in the center of a square formed of unhusked rice, having at its four corners four water pots encircled five times with cotton thread. The next ceremony is *Mutyalapolu* which resembles *Mylapolu*, except that the bridal pair, seated inside, are made to worship their tutelary deity, Virabhadra. After *Jiragudam, Kankanam* and *Podghattanam* have been performed, as is coustomary among the other Telugu castes, the *Puste* or the auspicious necklace is tied around the bride's neck and *Mattelu* are put on her toes. Then comes *Kanyadanam* or the formal gift of the bride to the bridegroom by her parents, which constitute the essential portion of the ceremony. Under *Pota*, the caste people are entertained at a feast, while under *Tota*, the bridal pair are entertained at a garden party and subsequently carried in procession to the temple of the village Hanuman. On the *Nagavelly* day, the bridegroom holds a sword, in his hand and the couple walk three times round twenty one leaf plates arranged circularly, each containing a heap of cooked rice with a dough lamp on its top. A brahmin usually officiates as priest at the ceremony, otherwise Jangam's services are engaged for the purpose[28].

Widows are allowed to marry again by the *Marumanuvu* ritual. This ceremony takes place at night. The bridegroom visits the bride's house, presents her with *sari, choli* and bangles and brings her with him to his house. Next day a feast is given to relatives and friends[29].

Divorce is recognised and effected, with the sanction of the caste *Panchayat*, by tying a rupee in the woman's garment and expelling her from the house. Divorced womens may marry again with in the caste by the same rites as widows. A woman, taken to adultery with a member of the caste, is punished with a fine, which is used to provide the caste people with a feast. Adultery with a man of low caste entails expulsion from the caste.

The dead are disposed of by burial, being laid in the grave in a sitting posture, but unmarried persons are buried in lying position. In the former case a *Lingam, Vibhuti* (*ashes*) and *Bel* leaves are placed in the hands of the corpse. No mourning is observed nor sradha performed ; but on the 10th day after death caste people are fed in honour of the deceased. In the dark half of the month of *Bhadrapada* (September) offerings are made to departed ancestors in general through the agency of Jangams, who are fed and given presents.

Now some members of the caste have settled down to agriculture and are engaged as farm labourers. We find them in entire Telangana, Rayalaseema and East Godavari, West Godavari, Krishna, Guntoor, Nellore and Vishakhapatnam districts in Andhra Pradesh.

Kapu, Kamma, Reddy and Velama Communities

Pichikuntlas

The Pichikuntlas take donations from Kapu, Kamma, Reddy, Velama and Yadava castes by reciting their *Gotras* and family histories. Pichikuntla is derived from *Bikshakuntla*.(*Biksha* means begging and *Kuntla*-lame). Palkuriki Somana described the Pichikuntlas as physically handicapped who take donations from the *Sudra* community[30]. Narayanamatya refers to Pichikuntlas in his work *Hamsavimsati*. B. Ramaraju writes that the word *Pichuka* is derived from *Bikshaka* and Pichikuntla is thus, derived from *Bikshakuntla*. He also states that the *Bikshakuntla* is a well known nomadic tribe in Telangana districts even today[31].

There are two legends about the orgin of this caste. According to one legend a gotra reciter was required on the occasion of the weddings of the three primeval pairs, Vishnu and Laxmi, Brahma and Saraswathi, and Siva and Parvathi. One was created from a clay-image with a maimed leg. The descendants of this lame man have since been designated as Pichikuntla, or lame beggars, and follow the profession of genealogists or *gotra-reciters* to the Kapu and Golla castes.

Another legend speaks of seven Golla women being childless invoked god Siva for progeny. They were given a lame male infant to be brought up. In course of time the women also conceived by the grace of God, and delivered seven daughters who at the God's command were given in marriage to the lame boy. He was, there upon, provided with a *Shankha* (conch-shell), *Ghanta* (bell), *Yeddu* (Bull) and *Gajasulam* (an iron bar) and enjoined to lead a mendicant's life, going round on the bullock's back. His progeny were known as the Pichikuntlas[32]. Whatever light these legends throw upon the origin of the caste, it seems not improbable that the Pichikuntlas were the illegitimate descendents of the Kapu and Golla castes. There is no *Puranic* evidence in support of these legends. The Pichikuntlas are believed to be the offsprings of Golla and Kapu castes[33], because they are generally associated with these castes and recite their *gotras*.

In Karnataka, the population of Pichikuntlas is sizeable and they are called *Helavalu* (physically handicapped). They migrated to Karnataka from Andhra Pradesh. At first they were attached themselves to the Golla caste and later associated with the Kapus. They narrate not only the stories of the Kapu and Golla but also the other stories like *Palanati Veera Charitra, Kunti Malla Reddy Katha, Balanagamma Katha*, etc., to earn their livelihood.

According to 1981 Census the population of the Pichikuntlas was around 5,096. In Andhra Pradesh there are a number of sub-sects within Pichikuntla community[34] who depend upon the Reddy and Golla communities for their livelihood. The important sub-sects are *Katthi, Ghanta*, *Golla* and *Thuraga*. Among them the *Katthi* and *Titthi* Pichikuntlas visit the houses of the Reddys, the *Ghanta* Pichikuntlas visit Kamma houses, and the *Thuraga* and others visit Golla houses in Andhra Pradesh. But one Pichikuntla family should not go for taking donations to all the above communities. There are separate Pichikuntla families to take donations from *Matati* Reddys and Peda Kanti Reddys. We can see this difference in Siddareddy Gudem of the Khammam district, where nearly one hundred *Motati* Reddy and *Pedakanti* Reddy families are residing. The *Titthi* Pichikuntlas who hail from Jonnalagadda and Ambarupeta villages of Khammam district take donations from *Motati* Reddys. The *Katthi* Pichikuntlas who hail from Buchi Reddy Palem and Mamunoor villages take donations only from *Pedakanti* Reddys. These nomadic tribes of Pichikuntlas go to their respective Reddy families at different fixed times.

The Pichikuntlas of the Macherla village of Guntur district take donations only from Kammas[35]. The Pichikuntlas of Mukundapuram near Kodhada, Nalgonda district take donations only from Gollas but not from Reddys and Kammas. Thus, there are different sects in the Pichikuntlas and they depend upon their different patron communities. All the sub-sects have their own patron communities in the society. They have a clear code of conduct which has been followed by all the sub-sects since times immemorial. In accordance with the code of conduct, one sub-sect is authorised to take donations only from a particular patron community.

Pichikuntlas have *Mirasi* villages in Telangana, Andhra and Rayalaseema areas. They have a tradition to transfer their own *Mirasi* villages to others when they are not able to visit villages[36]. Pichikuntlas generally go round for taking donations after Sankranthi festival because the patron-community (Reddys) mainly belong to the agriculture profession and get crops by that time.

Every Pichikuntla troupe possesses a copper plate inscription as proof of their authority to take donations while they go to the Gollas and Reddys entertaining them with the recitals of the stories of *Kunti Malla Reddy Katha* and *Palanati Veera Charitra*. On the copper plate the *Dharmasasanam* is inscribed. It states that the Gollas and Reddys should donate alms to Pichikuntlas obeying this *Dharmasasanam*.

Pichikuntlas visit their respective areas (*Mirasis*) once in 3 years with their families and recite the stories of *Kunti Malla Reddy Katha* using the musical instruments. Touring the *Mirasi* villages is necessary for their living. They stay in each village for about 10 to 15 days and recite the stories. They build temporary huts and camp at one village and go to the neighbouring villages where the Golla and Reddy families reside in good number. Depending on the strength of the Golla and Reddy families in a village they stay in that village, even upto 6 months reciting the stories.

The troupe of Pichikuntla performers consists of three members. One is the main singer and the other two are supporting artists. The main singer wears a white lower garment (*Dothi*) shirt and a turban over his head. He holds a long sword and *Dalu* (shield).

His ornaments include ear rings with large ear studs of red stones, a nose ring, a silver chain around the neck. The supporting singers stand on either side of the main singer. They also dress like the main singer except the long sword and *Dalu* (shield). Accompanying singers play *Titthi* or Hormonium and *Dakki* (a small drum). Pichikuntlas pray Goddess Sharada, lord Ganapathi[37], Chennakeshavaswamy and also pray to the local gods and goddesses before they start the main story.

Pichikuntlas narrate not only the stories of Reddy community but also the other stories like Palanati Veera Charitra, Balanagamma katha and the stories related to the Mahabharatha to entertain their patron-community.

In the Pichikuntla community child marriages are common. Performing marriage of girls before puberty is considered more respectable. Girls, for whom husbands cannot be procured, are dedicated to the deities Ellamma, Mallanna and Rajeshwara. In theory, polygamy is allowed without any restriction. But having more than two wives is not a common practice.

Widows and divorcees may re-marry but such women are not permitted to participate in the family rituals or religious ceremonies on equal footing with the first wife. Divorce is permitted on the grounds of adultery or refusal to live together. The ritual observed at the time of granting divorce consists of breaking her string of black beads (*mangala sutra* or *puste*) and turning her out of the house.

Pichikuntlas are almost all Saivaites (*Vibhutidharies*) and worship Mallikarjuna as their patron god with offerings of sweet meats. Pochamma, the goddess who controls small pox as they believe is worshipped on Wednesdays with sacrifices of goats and fowls. Their other deities are (1) Ellamma, to whom they sacrifice fowls on Thursdays and Fridays, (2) Idamma, appeased with the offerings of goats on Wednesdays and (3). Maisamma, to whom goats and fowls are offered on Sundays. These offerings are later eaten by the members of the house hold. They strongly believe in witch-craft and spirits and when illness befalls on a family, the members seek the assistance of an *Erukala* woman to identify the troubling spirit and appease it with a variety of animal and other offerings. The functions of the priest are performed by Jangams, to whom great reverence is paid by the members of the caste[38].

As a rule Pichikuntlas bury their dead, the corpse being laid in a grave in a sitting posture facing the north, with *Vibhuthi* in one hand and a lingam in the other. After the grave is closed a temporary earthen platform is built over it *Nandi* or the figure of a bull is placed on all corners. On the 10th day after death the chief mourner worships the bulls and afterwards gets his head tonsured. Jangams conduct the funeral service and receive presents of rice and money. Departed ancestors in general are propitiated in the latter half of the month of *Bhadrapada* known as Mahalaya Paksha. Female ancestors are honoured by the women of each family in the form of earthen vessels designated Balamma.

We find Pichikuntlas in Warangal, Khammam, Ranga Reddy, Nalgonda and Guntoor districts, always moving from place to place for their livelihood.

Yadava Community

Mandahechus

The Mandahechus sing not only to entertain Golla community, but also to narrate the history of their ancestors. They record and preserve the history of their caste from generation to generation in oral form.

The Mandahechus[39] are also called Mandapichollu, Mandechulu, Manduchcha, Mandahechu, Bommalata Vallu, Podapothula, Podapothram, Pogadapotharlu, Podarulu etc., in Andhra Pradesh. By profession, all are mendicants belonging to the Golla community but have different names in different regions and zones. Their main occupation is reciting of *Katamaraju stories*, which are familiar as *Yadava Puranam* (or *Yadupuranam*) and take donations only from the Gollas. Besides story telling they demonstrate clay toys and sing lyrics and participate in the rituals of *Bonalu* (offerings) to the Goddess Ganga, the main deity of the

Golla community[40]. Katamaraju stories have become popular on account of Mandahechus. They have developed artistic skills in telling these stories more interestingly.

There are many legends in vogue regarding the origin of Mandahechus of which two are prominent. According to Keshavulu[41], Gollas were vegetarians and teetotallers in the ancient times. Hence when a sacrifice was to be performed, nobody came forward from any of the Golla tribes except *Alagolla* tribe. He killed the lamb by biting its neck with teeth and spilled the blood around the flock of sheep. This ritual is called *Gavu*. As a result it is believed that the *Manda* (the flock) had increased considerably. From then onwards the *Alagolla* were termed as Mandahechus for having increased the flock.

According to another legend, once upon a time many a sheep died mysteriously in Nellore region. Then Katamaraju got a net spread over the sheep and asked one of the Gollas to perform *Gavu* (*Bali*). Since they never used to eat meat, the Golla who performed *Gavu* came to Katamaraju and asked him for food with a blood mouth. Katamaraju despised him and excommunicated him from the tribe for his behaviour. When his livelihood became a problem he was allowed to takedonations for his food from his own community. Thus, a new parasitic nomadic tribe had emerged which started praising the valour of Katamaraju.

Any way, Mandahechus even today perform *Gavu* on the flock of sheep. After the narration of Katamaraju stories on the last day they pray to Goddess Ganga and then perform *Gavu*. Mandahechus perform *Gavu* in the early morning around 4.00 a.m. The performer is almost nude and cover himself with leaves. They make a couple of rounds around the flock and chant *Raksha Mantra* and then perform the *Gavu*. They take the dead lamb with them to their huts. Gollas believe that with the sacrifice or *Bali*, the loss of livestock and epidemic disease etc., will be prevented and thereby the flock increases.

Nagamallu, another Mandahechu[42] narrates a different story regarding the origin of Mandahechus. Once upon a time, there was a flock of sheep in a village and a Golla was its owner. The Golla had illicit relation with a woman who belonged to *Sharadagallu* caste, who lived on the outskirts of the village. She became pregnant and the villagers ex-communicated her. However, she stayed on and delivered a male baby. Since the *Sharadagallu* ex-communicated her from their community, the Gollas out of compassion gave her a ram (*Podalunnapothu*) and a goat to her as means of her livelihood. With all kinds of troubles, the boy completed his childhood. Since he tended the ram, he was called as *Podapothuwadu* and *Mandawadu* as he lived near the *Manda* (the flock). His offsprings were popular as Podapothula Wallu, Mandahechollu. Even today Gollas respect Mandahechus or Podapothulawaru.

According to another legend, long ago, there was a war between Aadikeshavaraju and Peddiraju at Kandemondelakota. At that time Gangamma, the Goddess of Gollas, told her brother Pothuraju that she was going to Peddiraju's wife to inform her about his death and he should stay on gaurding the dead body. When Pothuraju asked her for his livelihood, she said that Gollas themselves would give him a *Pothu* (a ram) as *Musti* (alms) every year. The progeny of Pothuraju were called Pothurajuwallu[43].

These legends have been very popular for years. The Mandahechus are not a distinct and homogeneous community. That they are born of mixed parentage is a fact that the Mandahechus revealed in confidence. However, they claim to be of Golla stock. But Gollas do not allow the Mandahechus to enter their houses though they help them either by giving alms or sheep. This practice is still existing in Nalgonda, Warangal, Karimnagar and in some parts of Vishakapatnam, Srikakulam districts. Thus, the main profession of Mandahechus is to take donations from Gollas by reciting the Katamaraju stories and the genealogy of Gollas.

Rarely we come across any references to Mandahechus in literature. Ayyalaraju Narayanamatya while referring to the people of different castes who visited the temple on the day of fair, mentions the Gollas especially Mandahechus as one among them[44].

B. Rama Raju in his book, *Telugu Janapadageya Sahityam*, mentions that, in Telangana, Yerra Gollas, Mandahechus and Birannalawaru narrate the stories of Katamaraju[45]. Even though the Yerra Gollas can narrate all stories but the right to tell Katamaraju stories is reserved by *Mandahechus* only.

Syed Siraj-Ul-Hassan observes that the Madati, Payakani, Podapothula and Manda Gollas subsist by begging alms from the Yerra and other higher Golla tribes[46]. But in fact the Mandahechus approach invariably all the tribes of the Gollas for donations.

T. Subba Rao wrote about lyric singers of Katamaraju stories and mentioned about the various names of them in different parts of Andhra Pradesh. In Vishakhapatnam, Podapothulawaru sing the Katamaraju stories; in Kanigiri seema Kommulawaru sing the Katamaraju stories and are called *Yachakulu*; in Telangana they are called *Tera Cheera Baktulu* and Mandahechulu; in Rayalaseema, particularly in Kurnool Mandal, they are known as *Suddulannalu*[47].

G. Nagaiah stated that, in Telangana region, Mandahechus tell Katamaraju Kathalu and these performances are also called *Gollasuddulu*[48]. The *Gollasuddulu* word is derived from the *Golla Suktulu* and it is attached to the Katamaraju story tellers for this instance.

In Vishakhapatnam area, Podapothulawaru sing the Katamaraju stories and show wall hangings and curtains with the paintings related to Katamaraju Kathalu. But these are not *Teracheeralavallu* and not even *Pooja* Gollalu. Podapothulawaru are mixed parentage of Golla and Sharadakalla (Jangam caste) woman. And this Podapothulavallu are also called Mandahechulu.

With these opinions we may conclude that Mandahechus have different names in different parts of Andhra Pradesh but their social status or position in the society is the same and they live on reciting and singing Yadava stories in general and Katamaraju Kathalu in particular.

Every Mandahechu troupe possesses a copper plate (Fig. 1) as an authentication which they take alongwith them to show to the Gollas. The copper plate grant was given by Yadava king Katamaraju to a Mandahechu *Baktudu* on Shalivanhana Saka 1565 years of Chandramana. On the copper plate the *Dharmasasanam* is inscribed[49]. It states that all the 12 tribes of Gollas should respect Mandahechus. And they should donate alms to Mandahechus at the rate of one lamb if they have one *Manda* (flock of sheep) and one calf if they have 7 cows. No one should disobey this *Dharmasasanam*.

The explanation given by Keshavulu, a Mandahechu, that one, Bhaktiranna was sent by Katamaraju to Kasi to get copper for inscribing the *Sasana*. It also states that the Mandahechus got right to take donations as they perform *Gavu*. Almost similar explanation was given by Turpati Srisailam and Yadagiri, other respondents who were interviewed.

We find Mandahechus in Miriyalagudem, Suryapet, Bhuvanagiri, Ramannapet, Munugodu, Nakrakal, Chowtuppal, Huzurnagar, Nalgonda, Solipet project area in Nalgonda district of Andhra Pradesh. Though they permanently stay at the above mentioned villages, they move from place to place for livelihood.

Mandahechus of Miriyalagudem visit Burudaraopet village, Narasampet mandal of Warangal district to tell Katamaraju kathalu to *Sadnam* Gollas and *Erra* Gollas. They are called by two names at Warangal as Podapothulawallu and Mandahechuvallu.

We also find them in Medak, Siddipet, Jogipet, Sangareddi, Sadasivapet etc., in Medak district. They were called as Podapothulavallu at Chilakala area of Medak district.

Another troupe tour Achampet, Wanaparthi, Kalvakurthi, Shadnagar, Palamoor of Mahaboobnagar. They tour almost entire

Mahaboobnagar and also parts of Rangareddy district demonstrate clay toys while telling Katamaraju Kathalu.

We find them frequently and they are more popular in Telangana region, particularly in Warangal and Nalgonda districts. We scarcely find them in Vishakhapatnam, Vijayanagaram districts. They do not tour Krishna and Guntur districts.

They were not so popular in Srikakulam, Vishakhapatnam, Vijayanagaram districts and Rajahmundry area. They tour these places only once in 3 years. They are called Podapothulawallu. In Prakạsham and Nellore districts apart from these there are many other Golla *Yachakulu*.

Mandahechus tour their respective areas (*Mirasis*) once in 3 years and recite and sing Katamaraju Kathalu and Sri Krishna Leelalu. They move along with their family members and *Devasthalamu Petti* (a big box containing 100 to 200 colourful clay toys and musical instruments - Fig. 2). They demonstrate them and make commentaries. These colourful clay toys are moulded by *Nakasis* or *Chitrakaras* who are professional clay toy makers. We find *Nakasis* at Vemulavada and Siricilla villages in Karimnagar district and Cherial and Jangoan in Warangal district and at Nirmal in Nizamabad district.

Mandahechus are habituated to tour villages along with their families[50], goat, sheep and chicks. Tours are compulsory for their living. They stay in each village for about 15 to 45 days and recite Katamaraju Kathalu. They build temporary huts (Fig. 3) and camp at one village and go to the neighbouring villages where the Golla families reside in good number. Depending on the strength of Gollas, they stay at a village, even for 6 months.

The troupe members distribute the collections equally among themselves and lead a contended life. They have convention that each of these troupes have jurisdictional areas called *Mirasis*. They do not trespass into others jurisdiction without their permission. In case of disagreements the village council consisting of 5 members decides their disputes and imposes fines and punishments on the erring parties.

In the Mandahechus, both men and women work. Women usually play the role of *Vanthalu* with their melodious voice as their men recite the story with due seriousness. They also help in playing *Dolu* and *Talam*.

They are non-vegeterians. They eat meat and drink liquor. During leisure, they go out for hunting rabbits, birds etc., and share the food with the other people of their community.

They speak Telugu with a peculiar accent among themselves unlike other Telugu communities. Usually, they do not speak to others with that accent. Their way of expression is the same as that of *Budigajangas*. They have some kind of comparision and also similarities with *Budigajangas* in matter such as accent tradition and customs[51]

Generally Mandahechus go out for taking donations after *Dasara* and *Deepavali* festivals, and return to their native places by July with the onset of the monsoons. They attend the fairs, marriages of relatives and friends, celebrate festivals while they tour other villages for taking donations.

They do not entertain dowry in their marriage. The main qualification for a bridegroom is the knowledge of Katamaraju Kathalu and eligibility for a bride is to have melodious tone to sing the stories. They accept alliances from *Rachakoya*, *Katipapala*, *Sharadagallu, Balasanthu* and *Budigajangas* etc. One of them performs the role of a *Pujari* and conducts marriage by chanting some *manthras*. Before marriage, they celebrate Mutyalamma and Pochamma festivals and after marriage they offer food to all their relatives.

Festivals and Bonalu

They celebrate festivals like Gangalamma, Ellamma, Mutyalamma, Mallanna, Pochamma, Sammakka, etc. in the Telugu month *Shravana* (roughly July - August). They also celebrate other festivals commemorating the Yadava heroes.

They perform *Bonalu* for Sammakka and Pochamma in the same month. During these functions, they bring two new pots and cook offerings to Sammakka and Pochamma. They keep one pot over the other and decorate them with crisma and turmaric powders. They keep oil-lamp on the pots and Mandahechu women carry them on their heads, to the respective temples. Their men will be wearing shorts, they dance and play drums with undressed hair on the way to the temples along with their women. In front of Sammakka temple, they keep *Bonalu* and offerings are made to Sammakka. They break a coconut and offer a hen as *Bali*. This kind of *Bonalu* festival is celebrated regularly in the month of *Shravana* every year.

Disputes within the Community (*Kula Panchayat*)

Like Gollas, Mandahechus also have separate caste *Panchayats* for resolving the disputes within their community. The members are punished for disobeying the elders or for not following the jurisdictional limits. The *Panchayats* can impose a fine upto Rs.500/- plus *Panchayat* expences failing which the member will face ex-communication. If any troupe enters into a village other than the prescribed one they should pay Rs. 500/- plus half of their earning to the other troupe of the Mandahechus to whom the village belonged[52]

At first these Mandahechus visit the house of head of the Gollas (*Golla Pedda*) of their *Bikshaka Mirasi* village. He (the Golla *Pedda*) arranges for thier stay and board. The following day they make rounds in the Golla streets playing music with *Dolu* and *Kommulu* etc. In this process they take help of the *Uoori Golla* (one of the local *Golla*). All Gollas will be assembled at the *Pedda* Golla's (Headman) residence and they decide about the donations or alms to be given. Later, Mandahechus start *Katamaraju Kathas* in the premises of Pedda Golla house. To complete the whole cycle of Katamaraju Kathalu it takes about 2 months. But usually they do not tell all the stories in single instalment. The Golla hosts decide how many stories are to be recited and other related matters.

Mandahechus recite the stories of chivalry and worriorship. However, romantic and comic elements also find place in their recital. We can also notice the philosophies of Saivisam and Shakti cult from their stories.

Dress of the Mandahechus

The main singer of *Mandahechus* wear a white lower garment (*Dothi*), a shirt and a turban over his head (Fig. 4). He holds a stick of one or half yard long with silver knobs at either ends. His ornaments include ear rings with large ear studs of red stones; a nose ring; a silver chain around the neck; *Gajjelu* (an anklet or gridle of small bells) to legs; *Ponchu* (a thick silver bangle) to right wrist; two silver bracelets on two hands; silver or copper rings to fingers; *Mattelu* (toe rings), *Bedi* (anklet) to right leg (Fig. 5). Generally the main singers have a long hair like that of ladies and tieup the hair (like *koppu*). They put on a black broad *Bottu* (vermillion mark on forehead) and Kajal to eyes. Supporting singers stand on either side of main singer. They also dress like that of the main singer except the stick with a silver knob. *Wanthala women* (side singers) play cybals or Harmonium.

Musical Instruments

Mandahechus use many musical instruments (Fig. 6) like *Napera* or Trumpet (usually made of Bronze), a small handy drum, a big *Dolu* (huge sized drum), large sized cybals, one *Ranabheri* (a kind of drum), Harmonium, *Thrishulam* with bells and Maddela (drum). Some even use *Dolu, Thithi, Talalu* of Gangireddulu vallu. Some Mandahechus use *Nagara* along with *Napera*. During performance one uses *Nagara* and other one blows *Napera*. Mandahechus believe that both *Nagara* and *Napera* are signs of Yadava kings. Some of them use even *Maddela* (drum). All the above mentioned musical instruments are used by almost all the troupes of Mandahechus, while narrating Katamaraju Kathalu.

Beginning of Katha Kathanam

Mandahechus pray Goddess Sharada, Donakoda Ganga, Ganapathi, Srikrishna, Mallanna (Lord Siva) of different holy places and also pray for local gods and goddesses. Some Mandahechus also sing some petty songs along with the *Wanthalu*, (side singers) before they start on the main story. Katamaraju katha is a lengthy lyrical ballad. It begins with Avula Valuraju (grand father of Katamaraju) and covers 3 generations till Katamaraju, consisting of about 32 stories in all. All these are properly interlinked with one another and give a full accout of the history of Yadava chiefs.

At the concluding night session, the Mandahechus pray to Goddess Ganga near the flock of sheep. Yadavas go to their flock with *Bonalu* (boiled rice oblation) and offer it to Goddess Ganga Devi. Later, in the early hours at about 4 A.M., the Mandahechus perform *Gavu*, then they collect the donations from the Yadavas and move to the other village.

Mandahechus tell other stories also. On the occasion of death of a Yadava elder, they tell stories in the memory of the elders who passed away. They take the clothes and shoes of the deceased and collect some money. It is their *Bikshaka* tradition.

By chance, in any village, if they do not get their demands fullfilled after the story telling, they make effigy of the defaulters and exhibit it to the Yadava community of other village to insult them.

Vishwabrahmin Community

(i) Runzas

Runzas are mendicants, who beat a drum called Runza and take donations only from the Kamsalis[53] and others of that class. They take donations from the people of five professions namely, carpenters, blacksmiths, bronzesmiths, goldsmiths, and sculptors. These five professions are collectively called as *Panchanamvaru* or *Vishwabrahmins*. Runzas are also called Rudramaheswarlu, Rudrangulu[54], Avajagallu[55] in Telugu. They are skilled in their performances of singing while playing on Runza. They give performances in the houses of their patron community i.e. Vishwabrahmins.

Runza is a musical instrument. For this word 'Runza', several meanings like *Danguramu*, *Veeranamu*, *Rounza* are offered in the Telugu dictionaries[56]. Adibatla Venkataramana explained about Runza, that "there is a mention of Runza in *Andhra Basha*

Bhushanam. Avajamu, Runza, Danguramu, Veeranamu are different synonyms for Runza"[57]. Ayyalaraju Narayanamatya in his *Hamsavimsati* made use of two words *Avajamu* and *Veeranamu* as the synonyms of Runza, while describing the festivities at the fair in the thirty-nineth day story[58]. Runza is mentioned in Telugu literary works and inscriptions from 10th and 11th century onwards. Especially in the inscriptions of the Kakatiyas Runza is mentioned very often. In the inscription of a village Durgi, situated 10 km away from Macherla taluq of Guntur district, the name of the *Avajakadu* is mentioned at two or three places. Suryarayandra dictionary and Sabdaratnakaramu also offered the meaning of the *Avajakadu* as a musical instrument made of animal skin. Andhra vachaspatyam clearly mentioned the meaning of *Avaja* as Runza[59].

There is a legend about the origin of the Runza caste. According to that, Vishwakarma was requested to provide the drums for the marriage of Parvathi and Parameshwara. Then Viswakarma killed the giant called Rounjaka, made a Runza out of his skin and produced 32 kinds of melodious notes by playing on it. *Vishwakarma Puranam* explains that the marriage of Parvathi and Parameshwara was conducted with that Runza only. Since the skin of the giant Rounjaka was used, this instrument was named after the giant, and in course of time, it has been transformed into Runza[60].

Brass is also used in the making of Runza. Its height is about 3 or 3 1/2 feet. The upper part is covered with goat's skin, eleven holes are made above and below and eleven chords are tightly tied all over so as to make a sling, (*utti* in Telugu). The Runzas bend the instrument slantwise, press it firmly with the knee, and by pulling the strings with their hands and using slender bamboo sticks, produce musical notes rapidly. (Fig. 1).

Suravaram Pratapa Reddy in his Andhrula Sangeeka Charitra explained about the Runzas that, Runzas lived during Kakatiya period. Their name is mentioned in *Palanati Veera Charitra* and also in the writings of Palkurki Somanatha[61]. A scene of a woman playing on Runza is also seen inscribed in Nagarjuna Konda[62].

According to the 1891 census, the population of the Runzas was only 150. Their name was not registered as Runzas in the Madras census[63]. Even today their number ranges from 100 to 150.

Though some Runzas have landed property, their main profession is only playing on Runza. Along with education, they learn playing on Runza from their child hood. After learning the playing of Runza they go for taking donations. They set out in bullock-carts along with their families. They also keep the cooking ware with them on their visits.

On their visits to the villages they take donations only from Vishwabrahmins. They are respected and provided with grains and money as alms. By narrating stories, singing songs with the help of the Runza, they make the Vishwabrahmins happy. In their demonstrations they produce all the notes melodiously.

When they go to a village they beat Runza and make their presence known to the Vishwabrahmins. For one whole night they recite the story to the Vishwabrahmins explaining the lineage of the *Pancha Brahmanas* and their duties and also the importance of existance of our human body and five elements. *Pancha Brahmanas* mean *Manuvu, Maya, Thustna, Shilpa* and *Vishwagna*. They allocate different kinds of duties to *Pancha Brahmanas* - iron work to *Manuvu*, wood work to *Maya*, brass work to *Thustna*, stone work to *Shilpi* and gold work to *Vishwagna*. Then they applaud the significance of *Omkara*.

Of all the stories narrated by Runzas, *Parvathikalyanam, Dakshayajnam, Virabhadravijayamu, Vishwakarmapuranam* are worthy of mention. All these have 18 contos, full of Sanskrit slokas written in the form of books of palm leaf. Runzas explain that in the story of *Vishwakarmapuranam* the origin of Vishwa Brahmin caste and Vishwakarma's life along with the birth of the Universe.

Runza troupe consists of six members. Two members out of six, play on *Thalas* (cybols) and the other two members play on Runza, the remaining two members play on *Sonnai* or *Kommuburas* when they are reciting stories for Vishwabrahmins (Fig. 2). Generally Runzas go to the house of Vishwabrahmins for taking donations during the festival days of Sivaratri and in the months of *Kartika, Magha,* and *Vaishaka*. The system of playing Runza is still practiced in marriages of Vishwabrahmins and in temples. They never play the Runza and recite the stories in the streets and in the houses of other castes. Generally the Runzas recite the stories of *Parvathikalyanam* for 5 days. At the request of the host community, they recite it even for 10 days, otherwise they complete it in a single day. Runzas pray to goddess Shambavi before beginning the story of *Parvathikalyanam.* Then they sing a song in *Kalyani raga* with *Aditala* on goddess Kanchi kamakshi[64]. At the same time they also sing the eulogy of *Vishwakarma*[65]. Then they recite the *Parvathikalyanam* story for their audience. They also recite *Rounzakasuravadha* story to entertainment of their hosts.

In the Runza stories, they produce thirtyfive melodious notes on Runza in tune with the context. They also produce different sounds on Runza like that of army parade, horse hoofs, band marching and short drum. Thus, Runzas complete their story reciting with different types of slokas, songs, prose and sounds. Lastly, they offer *Mangalaharathi* at the end of the story. Then they take donations (*Thyagam*) from their patron caste Vishwabrahmin and leave for another village. Thus, they lead nomadic life in Andhra Pradesh.

Now-a-days Runzas appear in some places of Andhra Pradesh. Vibhuti Anjaneyulu in Srikakulam district, Pasham Palalochanudu and Gidikanthi Satyanarayana at Draksharamam in East Godavari district and Brahmanadham, Vaikuntam, Indrasena at Boyinapalli in Nalgonda district are well-known Runza drum beaters in Andhra Pradesh. They go on tour once in two or three years to their *Mirasi* villages.

They only take donations from their respective *Mirasi* villages and they do not venture to trespass into others villages[66]. If they do so that would be considered as a crime and they would be awarded punishments in *Kula panchayats* and penalties would be imposed on them.

They completely follow the Saivite tradition. Lord Siva and Vishwakarma are the main gods of Runzas. They never accept the superiority of other communities on their patron community. They never take donations from other communities expcept Vishwabrahmins. They celebrate all the festivals of their host community.

(ii) Panasavaru

Panasavaru also take donations only from Vishwabrahmins by reciting *Vishwakarmapuranam* on harmonium once in a year. Some times they recite the *Vishwakarmapuranam* and the *Gotras* in front of the houses of Vishwabrahmins and explain the different traditions followed by the different *Gotra* Vishwabrahmins on different occasions. Both Runzas and Panasas depend on Vishwabrahmins for their livelihood, but they have their respective *Mirasi* villages for taking donations in Andhra Pradesh.

There is a legend about the origin of the Panasa caste. According to it a girl was born out of a sacrificial fire (*Homagni*) with the divine power of Vishwakarma. By the *Maya* (power) of Vishwakarma the girl gave birth to a male child. As the child's mother had no milk, Vishwakarma created a creeper and produced milk from jack fruit. Since the boy drank that milk, he was named as *Panasavadu*. The progeny of the boy, in course of time were called Panasalu[67].

E. Thurston explained about Panasas. The Panasas are a class of beggers in the Telugu country, who take alms only from Kamsalis. The word Panasa means constant repetition of words, and, in its application to the Panasa, probably indicates that they, like the Bhatrazu bards and panegyrists, make up verses eulogising those from whom they beg. It is stated in the Kurnool manual (1886) that "they take alms from the Beri Komatis and gold smiths (Kamsalis) and no others. The story says that, in Golkonda, a tribe of komatis named *Bacheluvaru* were imprisoned for non-payment of arrears of revenue. Finding certain men of the artificer class who passed by in the street split betel nut, they got it in to their mouths and bagged the artificers to get them released. The artificers, pitying them, paid the arrears, and procured their release. It was then that the Kamsalis fixed a *vartana* or annual house fee for the maintainance of the Panasa class, on condition that they should not beg alms from the other castes[68]. Subbachary explained about two tribes in the Panasa caste, i.e., *Adi Panasas* and *Komati Panasas*[69].

Infact, the Panasas do not belong to the artist class. They recite only the *Gotras* infront of the houses of their hosts and take donations from them. They are Saivites. They are not seen without wearing Siva lingas. They compulsorily put sacred ash (*Vibhuti*) on their fore head and wear rosaries. They regard their benefactors as gods. At present their tradition is on the decline. According to 1891 census[70], the population of Panasas was only 52 in the Hyderabad state. It is not possible to get the exact number of Panasas because most of them claim their caste as Vishwabrahmins. Presently, the Panasa families can be seen only in Khammam of Telangana region. In other parts of Andhra Pradesh the number of their families is negligible.

Padmasali Community

Sadanasurulu

Sadanasurulu, who are also called Jugglers, take donations only from Padmasalis once in three years. They are also called *Sadanollu*. At present they are very less in number than Kunapulivaru who are also attached to Padmasali community. Now we find them only in Valbapoor, Huzurabad Mandal of Karimnagar district and in some parts of Medak districts.

E. Thurston explained the word Sadanasurulu and recorded a legend regarding the origin of the same. Sadanasura is recorded in the Madras Census Report of 1901, as synonym of *Samayamuvadu*. In a note on this class of itinerant mendicants, C. Hayavadana Rao states that, unlike the *Samayamuvaru*, they are attached only to the Padmasali section of the Sale caste. "They say" he writes that "their name is an abbreviated form of *Renuka Sakthini Sadhinchinavaru* i.e. those who conquered *Renuka Sakti*". According to the tradition, Renuka was the mother of Parasurama, one of the *avatars* of Vishnu and is identified with the goddess Yellamma, whom the Padmasalis revere. The Sadanasurulu are her votaries. Ages ago, it is said that they prayed to her on behalf of the Padmasalis, and made her grant boons to them. Since that time they have been treated with marked respect by the Padmasalis who pay them annually four *annas*, and give preferential treatment in their marriages[71], ceremonies and rituals.

There is another legend regarding the origin of the Sadanasurulu caste. According to it, once upon a time a giant Kaluvasura was harassing the people. Some persons from Sale community formed as a secret group to protect their community. They learned magic tricks and incantations to guard their families at nights. This group of people helped a lot in the battle field with their magic, when Bhavanarushi the founder of the Padmasali community waged a war against the Kaluvagiant. In recognition of the help rendered in the battle field by the group, Bhavanarushi named them as Sadanasurulu (which means *Sadinchinavaru*) and granted them a boon to take donations from Padmasalis by reciting their genealogies once in two years. From then onwards they became dependant caste of the Padmasali community[72].

Parvathalu[73], narrated another legend regarding the origin of the Sadanasurulu. According to it, once upon a time, there was a king by name Krishna Gandhava, ruling his kingdom with a fort called *Ontisthambam Meda*. He did penance and prayed to Goddess Kalika Devi to grant a boon to him to rule 56 kingdoms on his own and to live forever. The goddess appeared before him and granted the first desire. Regarding the second desire, the goddess asked him to sacrifice every day a person and a piece of new cloth for a period of 12 years. From then onwards the king Krishna Gandhava started sending a man everyday from each family of his 56 kingdoms and praying to Goddess Kalika Devi with a new cloth taking from

Padmasali community. People were not aware of the fact that their king was worshipping of goddess, Kalikadevi daily with human sacrifice. The people were of the view that the persons, whom the king had taken from their families were living somewhere in the empire serving in the military. For this daily sacrifice many people were killed. In a few years, all the families except Padmasalis in his 56 kingdoms had contributed one male member in their families, but still some more years were left to complete the period of 12 years. Hence, the king asked each family to contribute another person. The people revolted against the king and asked him why he had taken one person from each family except Padmasali community. Then the king explained that Padmasali community was giving a new cloth every day all these years. Then the people expressed their opinion that they would also give new cloth hereafter and asked the king to take the persons from Padmasali community for his purpose. But Padmasalis did not agree to send a person from their families. So the king imprisoned all the Padmasalis for not obeying his orders.

The Padmasalis do not take food without taking bath and performing *Sandyavandanam* (Prayer at dawn, midday and dusk). So the Padmasalis in the jail gave 5 *Varahas* as a bribe to the Jailer and told him that they would return to jail after performing *Sandyavandanam*. The Jailer accepted and released them from jail. The Padmasalis went directly to the Bhavana Rushi and Markandeya temples and beat drums. Hearing the big sound, the people of 50 villages came to them. Then these Padmasalis explained to them the king's sacrifice and organized a meeting to take a decision. All the Padmasalis came to an agreement that the person who comes forward to kill the king would be honoured by entire community with *Bottu* betel (*Thambulam*) and other rituals. To protect the Padmasali community and the people, the Padmasalis, having the *Adepu, Ganji, Kudidhi, Bhandaru* as surnames, came forward from the crowd and took the oath to kill the king. Then the Padmasalis, who came from jail, perfomed *Sandyavandanam* and went back to jail.

As per the oath, the *Adepu, Ganji, Kudhidi* and *Bhandaru* Padmasalis dared to kill the king, Krishna Gandhava. But the king resides in seven storied building called *Ontisthambam meda*. On the way to the king's residence there was a river, Ganga. And near the residence there was Goddess Kalika devi. Seeing all these hurdles, they went to Gollaketamma, who knows magic. They learned magic from Gollaketamma and crossed the river to reach king's residence. There they saw Goddess Kalika Devi. Goddess Kalika ordered them to go back. Then these Padmasalis prayed to Kalika and told about their oath. Then Goddess Kalika put a test to Padmasalis. She asked them to drink toddy and eat meat in the pot. The Padmasalis did the same for the sake of fulfilling their vow. Thus, they learned the secret of king's death from the goddess and killed him using his own sword. They released all the imprisoned Padmasalis. Thus, they came to be called *Sadanasurulu* which means *Sadinchinavaru* in Telugu. Thereafter, these Padmasalis were honoured by the entire community with Rupees two from each family and the preferential treatment during the ceremonies in their houses.

Sadanasurulu take donations only from Padmasalis once in two years by performing magic tricks. They enter a village by beating a drum (Fig. 1 & 2) and stay in the village for three to seven days. They first visit the house of *Kulapedda* (head of community). Later, they go to all the Padmasalis by beating the drums. They perform all their magic tricks in the open place.

Magic tricks exhibited by Sadanasurulu

1. Jala sthambana

Sadanasurulu perform various feats before the people in the open place. ***Jalasthambana*** is one of them. In this a Sadanasurudu takes water with a pipe through one of his nostrils and releases it through another nostril. This performance is called ***Jalasthambana*** (Fig.3).

2. Agnisthambana

In this performance, Sadanasurulu select a person from audience and puts a clay hearth on his head and makes *puris* (Fig. 4) without causing any burn injury to the head of the person.

3. Addrushya sthambana

In this performance Sadanasurulu plant four bamboo sticks on four sides and cover them with a cloth, then they ask a person among the audience to come forward to tie the troupe leader with a rope to one of these bamboo stick. Later, they close the curtain. After some time, they open the curtain. Surprisingly, the person who was tied with a rope at one bamboo stick appears to be tied to another stick (Fig. 5). This performance is called *Addrushya sthambana*.

4. Bark Palanquin

In this performance Sadanasurulu construct palanquin with bark sticks. The troupe leader sits on it, the other members carry it on their shoulders to show the audience (Fig. 6&7). The palanquin bears the weight for the surpriseof the audience.

5. In another performance, the troupe leader sleeps on the floor. Four members collectively bring a big stone and put it on the chest of that leader. They start breaking the stone by using a big hammer without causing any injury to the troupe leader.

6. In another performance the troupe leader takes a pot and fills it with water. He mixes turmeric powder in it before the audience (Fig-8). After some time he produces dry turmeric powder again from the pot.

7. Two members of the troupe stand in the opposite direction before the audience at a distance of one yard. Each one takes a thin metallic plate in his hand. With the power of the sap of leaves in their hands the plates suddenly jump, dash each other and return to the same place.

Their performance lasts for three hours only during day unlike the performences of other communities. They bring along with them a copper plate in which *Dharmasasanam* is inscribed. After the completion of their performance they take donations from Padmasalis and go to another village. Thus, they tour all their *Mirasi* villages for their livelihood. Presently we find them in Valbapoor village, Huzurabad Mandal of Karimnagar district. Now there is only one family residing in that village.

Mutrasi Community

Pandavulavaru

Pandavulavaru or Pandavulollu take donations from Mutrasi community. This Mutrasis also called Mudiraj or Tenugu in Andhra Pradesh. Pandavulavaru recite the story of Pandavas, the heroes of the Mahabharatha period. That is why they are called Pandavulavaru[74]. While reciting the stories for Mudiraj community they play a musical instrument called *Kinnera* melodiously, and express all their gestures. They recite not less than 40 stories related to *Mahabharatha*. Among them the *Yayathicharitra* and the *Pandava Vanavasamu* are very important. The *Yayathicharitra* narrates the origin of Mudiraj community and the *Pandava Vanavasamu* narrates the origin of the Panadavulavaru. In the entire Telangana region Pandavula troupes invariably recite these two stories. The entire Mahabharatha story can be heard from them.

There is a legend regarding the origin of Pandavula caste. The legend is mentioned in *Pandava Vanavasamu* katha. According to it Jampanna and Duggana were guarding their cucumber garden in the outskirts of a village. They belonged to Mutrasi community. They thought that they would one day host the Pandavas. Wandering in the forest, one day, the Pandavas came to them. The Mutrasis hosted a feast to Pandavas who later constructed a hut at a short distance from the cucumber garden and lived for some time. One day Pandavas went for hunting in the forest and did not turn up till late in the night. Then Draupadi went to the forest in search of Pandavas and reached Mutrasis cucumber garden. Draupadi asked Dugganna, who was warming up himself by fire, about the Pandavas. Dugganna, with an intention to test Draupadi, told that the Pandavas were killed by a *Shakti* Goddess in the forest and he was performing funeral rites pretending his succession to them. There was a little bit of doubt in the mind of Dugganna regarding Draupadi. He thought that she might be a devil. That is why Dugganna told the lie. But

Draupadi believed it and put an end to herself. After some time Pandavas came to Dugganna. Dugganna told them about Draupadi. Then Dharmaraju became angry and killed Dugganna on the spot. After some time Jampanna came there and explained the truth that there was no mistake of his brother Dugganna. Then Dharmaraju meditated on Srikrishna and Dugganna came back to live. After that, Jampanna caused Draupadi to come to life. Later, Jampanna was nominated by Dharmaraju to be the village head while Dugganna became a mendicant repenting for his misdeed. Then Dharmaraju sent for palm leaves and wrote the entire story of the *Mahabharatha* on them and gave it to Dugganna to recite it. By reciting the story of *Mahabharatha,* the progeny of Dugganna became Pandavulavaru[75].

One Manikyam[76], who belonged to Pandavula community, gave a different account that they belonged to *Gondu* tribe. According to him the name of their caste is *Thotikulam*. The main profession of this tribe is to recite the stories from ancient times. The *Gondu* tribe lives in Adilabad district. Their main Goddess is *Nagoba*. The *Gonds* of Adilabad district also worship this goddess *Nagoba*. The Mutrasis in olden times were eking out their livelihood by collecting forest products and selling them in towns and villages. Perhaps this relationship might have tiedup the Mutrasis with the *Gondu* community. Thus, we may conclude that the Pandavulavaru belongs to *Gondu* tribe but they depend on *Mutrasi* community for their livelihood. Pandavulavaru recite *Yayathi Charitra* which describes the origin of their patron community. This is almost the same as *Yayathicharitra* in Telugu Mahabharatha. This legend also begins with the explanation of the creation of man.

Pandavulavaru usually recite the stories at nights but sometimes during day time also if required by their host community. They recite one story each day, from the Mahabharatha for 41 days. The main singer holds a *Kinnera* (Fig. 1) in his left hand, a ring in his right hand finger. He wears *Dhoti*, shirt and a rose colour head dress. The supporting singers stand on either side of the main singer wearing similar dresses. The right side singer plays on *maddela* and the left side singer beats cybols. The main signer also wears *Gajjelu* (an anklet or gridle of small bells) in his ankles. The main singer acts according to the story to attract the audience. At first they pray to Ganapathi, later, Saraswathi, and starts the main story. The story reciting is continued sometimes in prose too, some of the singers sing songs in the present day film tunes. Through this art form *Yayathi Charitra*, the caste legend of Mutrasis and *Pandava Vanavasakatha*, the caste legend of Pandavulavaru are being extensively popularised. Pandavulavaru have *Mirasi* villages in entire Telangana. They are found in Ranga Reddy, Warangal, Karimnagar, Adilabad and Nalgonda districts.

Manikyam, Laxmaiah, Eswaraiah, Hanumaiah, are well known singers in Attapuram of Rangareddy district. Ramulu, Ramaswamy, Narasimha, Kistaiah, are some well known singers of Pandavula tribe in Secundrabad area. In Warangal district Yadagiri, Satyanarayana, Saraiah, Bikshapathi, Narayana are famous singers. Agamaiah in Medak district and Yadagiri in Nalgonda district are also popular.

The Pandavula tribe follow different systems of marriage, one of them is *Voli* which means the sending of the bride to the grooms house where the marriage will take place. Usually the system is followed by the parents of the girl who could not afford to conduct the marriage at their residence. The economically poor families perform the marriage of their daughters with a turmeric root tied to the yellow thread (*Pasupukommu*) and the affordable people use two small gold discs (*pusthelu*) in the *mangalasutram*. The system of re-marriage is in vogue in their caste. Prostitution and theft are rarely found in this tribe. A fine of rupees 12/- is levied on the spouse, if he or she commits an immoral act. There is a system called *Pullaviruchuta* in their tribe. It is like divorce. While granting divorce, son is given to the mother and daughter to the father. The person who commits a serious mistake is imposed a fine of Rs. 600/-. If it is a very serious crime, he would be hit with *Sandals* (footwear) and penalty would also be collected from him.

The people of this tribe are Vaishnavites. They celebrate Ellamma and Pochamma festivals along with Dasara, Deepavali and Ugadi. They burn the dead bodies. They are non-vegetarians. They eat meat of squirrel, guana, pig, fish, mungoose, tortoise, rats, sparrow, rabbit, carls etc. We find different types of hunting tools and nets in their houses.

They usually speak in a different language called *Thoti* which has no script. They converse in this language among themselves. But they speak in Telugu with others.

Kummari Community

(Potters)

Pekkaras (Kulam Biddalu)

Pekkaras take donations from Kummari (potters) community only. They recite the origin, evolution and *gotras* of potters caste. They are also called *Pekkerlu, Pekkarollu, Pekkandru* and *Kulam Biddalu*[77] in Telugu speaking areas. Now their number is very meagre. They bring palm leaf manuscripts related to *Kummari Gunda Brahma Puranam*, *Salivahanacharitra* and the gotras of potters (Fig. 1). They also bring a book along with them in which the names of the heads of the potters' families of their respective *Mirasi* areas are written (Fig. 2). They visit their *Mirasi* villages for taking donations once in two or three years from potters. In the areas of Vishakapatnam, Vijayanagaram, Srikakulam and Godavari districts the Pekkaras are called *Kulam biddalu* and in the rest of Andhra Pradesh they are called *Pekkarollu*. Since the Pekkaras claim themselves as Potters, their community was not separately mentioned in the 1891 census[78].

There is a legend regarding the origin and evolution of Pekkaras. According to it there were four brothers in a family. They collected some clay from a river bed which was situated in the outskirts of a village and divided it into four parts and kept it there itself on the bank of the river. The four brothers used to bring some amount of clay for making pots to sell. But one of the brothers who had a large family, had stolen some of the clay of the other brothers. Thereafter the other brothers appointed a guardian, who caught the other one, while stealing the clay. Later, a *Kula Panchayat* was held in which the brother, who was responsible for that robbery was ex-communicated from the caste. But later, he was allowed to beg from the community for his survival. The progeny of this family are called Pekkaras[79]. Even today the Pekkaras are not allowed near the houses of the potters, but they offer meals to them in the open yard in front of their houses at the clay heap. At the time of auspicious occasions like marriage the Pekkaras are not allowed at the Kummari houses as they are considered socially inferior to them.

Pekkara troupe consists of five members. They follow the method of *Yakshagana* in their performance. A drum called *maddela*, harmonium and cybols are their musical instruments. Each family of the potters in a village, usually offers one time meals and Rs. 10 to 20 to the troupe during the days of their performance.

There is a tradition among the potters' family that each potter (who is in possession of a *sare*, potter's wheel) is bound to offer donations to the Pekkaras. The potters who refuse to give donations would be subjected to insult and condemnation by the Pekkaras who make their effigies and exhibit at every other house, abusing them in filthy language.

Medicherla Rajalingam, Venkateshwara Rao, Suryanarayana, Appala Raju, Eluru Suryanarayana, Senigarapu Krishnamurthy, Buggala Rama Rao and Satyanarayana are some famous Pekkaras who visit the potters' houses. They are all residents of Chintalapudi village, Thirumaladevipeta Mandal of West Godavari district.

Like potters, Pekkaras are also Saivites. They pray to Lord Siva every day before going to work. The Pekkaras collect some grain and Rs. 1000 to 1500 for their visit once in two or three years from the village. Generally they visit their *Mirasi* villages after Sankranti festival and stay in every village for 10 to 15 days. They move from one village to another for their livelihood.

In the modern times, the families of this community have mostly abandoned their traditional profession and took to some other jobs. Now they are found in Janga Reddy Gudem, Tirumaladevipeta of West Godavari district and in the outskirts of Vijayawada.

Madiga Community

Chindus: (Chindu Madigas)

Chindu Madigas depend on Madiga community only. They are also called *Sindollu, Chindubagothulavaru* and *Chindu Madigas*. The *Sindollu*, *Chindiwandlu*, or *Bogam Madiga*, are the courtesans of the Madiga caste; they attend to all Madiga ceremonies and entertain them by songs and dance. They maintain themselves by prostitution also. Their name *Sindi*, or *Sindollu*, is said to have derived from *Sairandhri*, the Sanskrit word for a lady hair stylist[80]. They mainly recite *Jambava Puranam* to Madigas in which they trace the origin and evolution of the Madiga community. They also recite not less than 50 stories related to the *Mahabharatha*, *Ramayana* and *Bhagavatha*. According to the wish of the host community they recite one story each day up to fifty days. *Mohinirukhmangada katha, Sarangadhara, Chenchu Laxmi, Virabhimanya, Mairavana, Śri Krishna rayabharamu, Alliranikatha, Satya Harichandra, Krishnarjuna Yuddam, Sathisavitri* and *Gayopakyanam* are important stories narrated by the Chindus.

Chindu Bhagavatam is a unique folk-drama presented by the Chindu Madigas. It is a tradition in Chindu Madiga community that every member of the family must play *Bhaghavatam* in praise of the Lord through song and dance. The costumes and make-up in *Chindu Bhagavatham*, to some extent resembles *Vidhinatakam* and *Yakshaganam*[81]. But the *abhinayam* i.e. gesticulation of limb movements of the Chindu artists is quite different. Another special feature of *Chindu Bhagavatham* is that all characters are present on the stage irrespective of the scene. The orchestra players also assist them in singing. When the king's role or Narasimhaswamy's role is presented on the stage some inflammable chemical (generally used in fire crackers) is thrown on the burning torches on both sides of the stage for creating flashes of light. The ornaments like *Bhujakirtulu* (shoulder decorations) *Kiritam* (crown) and *Tarahaaraalu* (Necklaces) of glittering tinsel and artificial beads, sparkle brilliantly causing astonishment and amusement to the folks. One more peculiarity of Chindu *Bhagavatam* is that the players are always active on the stage. They continuously dance or move their limbs[82] to attract the attention of the spectators always.

They visit Madiga houses once in two years. They mainly recite *Jambava Puranam* to them by constructing a dais in open place near the head of the Madiga caste. Their art form is called *Chindu Yakshaganam*. This *Yakshagana* method is very famous in the Telangana districts. We find the Chindu troupes of national and international fame in Nizamabad district of Telangana. The Nizamabad troupe got national reputation in reciting *Sarangadhara Katha* in the *Yakshagana* method. The most important aspect of their performance is that each and every member can play any character or role in the story which they recite. The *Jambava Puranam* is common to both Malas and Madigas. Malas and Madigas both sit in the audience. A Jester opens the show and announces the details of the programme for the day. He continues on the stage from the beginning to end and introduces the characters to the audience whenever a character comes on to the stage for the first time in the play. Besides this, he also takes part in singing and dancing with all the characters on the stage. Their narration of the story includes poetry, prose, and songs. Women also participate in the performance.

The Chindu Madigas *Jambava Puranam* recitation depends on two important roles i.e. one *Brahmin* role (*Gosangi*) and other Jambavantha. The subject of the conversation of these two roles constitute *Jambava Puranam*.

Radha Krishna Murthy described about *Yakshagana Prakriya* and *Chindu Madigas*. According to him the Telugu speaking area was called *Yakshabhoomi* in ancient times because the *Yakshas* who belonged to *Gandarva* race were known for their music and dance. This *Yakshagana* has been easily understood by the village folk and it is being performed since ages[83].

The Terracotta exhibits which the troupe carries with them

Drum beating

(Courtesy : School of Folk and Tribal Lore
P.S. Telugu University, Orugallu campus, Warangal)

Jalasthambana Performance

(Courtesy : School of Folk and Tribal Lore)

Traditional Viramusti with his customary dress, other decorations and weapons

The Prabhas

The Prabhas going in procession

Viramustis going to the Vaisya households to take donations

Viramusti performing Narasa

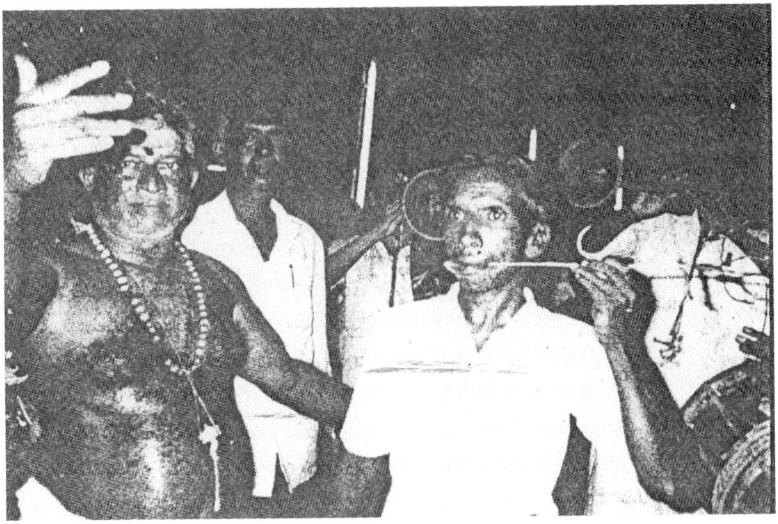

Viramusti performing Narasa

Viramusti performing Narasa

Performance of Pichikuntlas

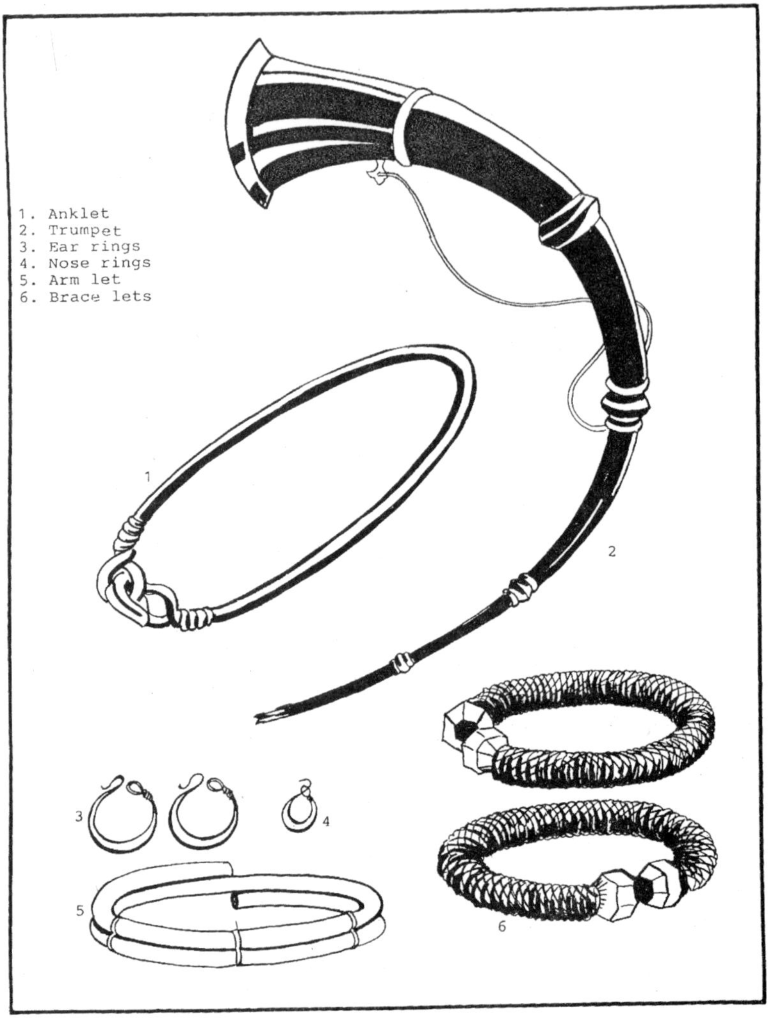
1. Anklet
2. Trumpet
3. Ear rings
4. Nose rings
5. Arm let
6. Brace lets
1
2
3
4
5
6

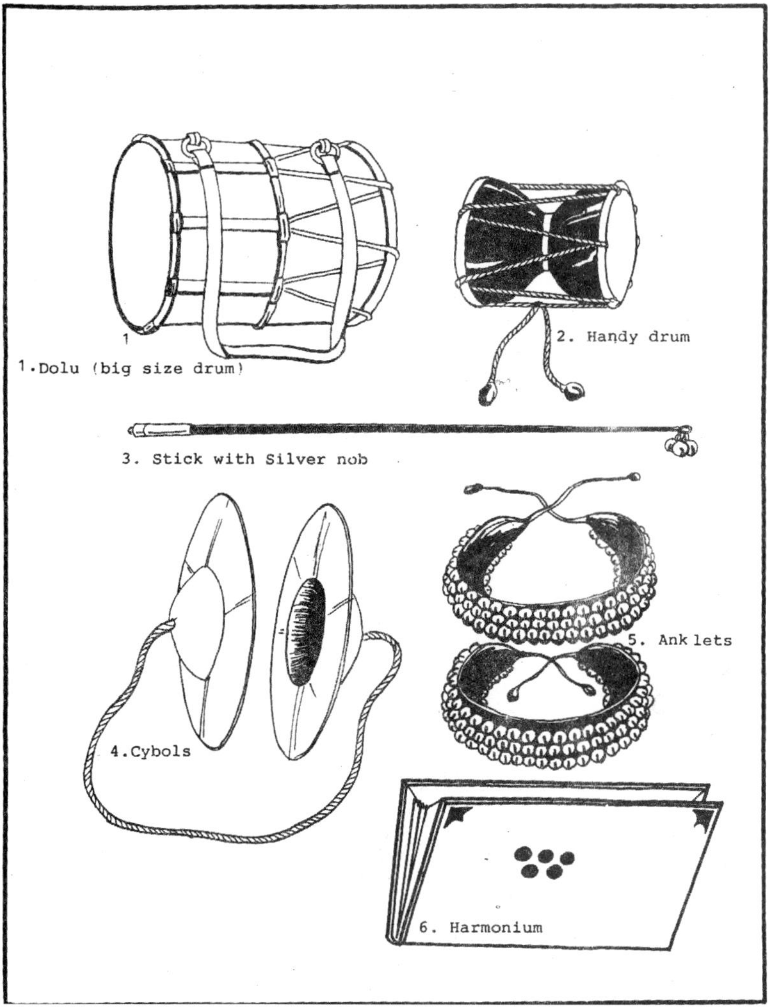
1
1.Dolu (big size drum)
2. Handy drum
3. Stick with Silver nob
4.Cybols
5. Ank lets
6. Harmonium

Runza drum beater

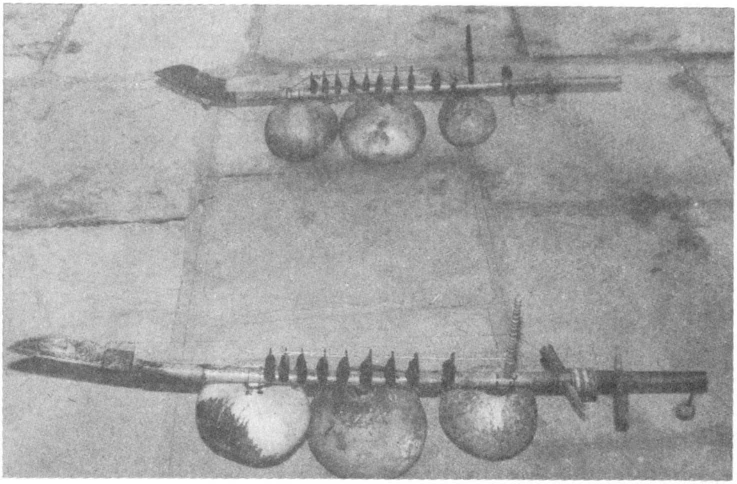

Kinnera
Musical instrument of Pandavulavaru
(Courtesy : School of Folk and Tribal Lore)

Troupe Members of Pandavulavaru
performing the Bhimanjaneya yuddam
(Courtesy : School of Folk and Tribal Lore)

Copper Plate Grant of Pandavulavaru
(Courtesy : School of Folk and Tribal Lore)

The palm leaf manuscripts of
Kummari Gundaiah Puranam and Salivahana Charitra

Make-up of Chindu Bhagothulavaru

Savitri and Yamadharmaraja in
Satisavitri stage performance
(Courtesy : School of Folk and Tribal Lore)

Kadem Sammaiah troupe

Narayanapur, Palampet, Warangal district

Yamadharma Raja in
Satisavitri stage performance
(Courtesy : School of Folk and Tribal Love)

Patam of Patamuvaru
Anustanam

(Courtesy : School of Folk and Tribal Lore)

Copper Plate Grant of Patamuvaru
Side-A

(Courtesy : School of Folk and Tribal Lore)

God Katamaiah

Karnekanti Gopal
Dakkali troupe leader as Siva in
Jambava Puranam performance

Agnisthambana Performance
(Courtesy : School of Folk and Tribal Lore)

Addrushyasthambana Performance
(Courtesy : School of Folk and Tribal Lore)

Bark Palanquin
(Courtesy : School of Folk and Tribal Lore)

Patam of Kunapulivaru
Sayampeta village, Warangal district

Patam of Goudajettis

Surabhandeshwara Katha

Patam of Dakkali Namadic Tribe

Chindu Madiga troupes generally present their performances during the harvest season, staying for 4 to 5 days in a village. On the final day they collect their donations and move to another village. They have *Mirasi* villages in Telugu speaking areas. We find them in the three regions of Andhra Pradesh, i.e. Telangana, Rayalaseema and Andhra.

Chindu troupes belonging to Nizamabad, Adilabad, Karimnagar and Medak districts of Telangana areas are very famous. In Nizamabad district we find a number of Chindu troupes who are well known in Andhra Pradesh. In the Nizambad district Armoor troupe has a special place among all the troupes of Chindus. They gave performances throughout India. They were given many awards by different social and cultural organisations. In this troupe, Chindula Yellamma is the most reputed actress[84]. She made a mark in this art for playing different roles superbly. She is a robust lady above seventy years by now but plays the roles of heroes and heroines, young and old with equal facility and efficiency. Usually she plays the role of Chitrangi in the story of *Sarangadharakatha* which gave her national reputation. She got many awards from different organisations including Andhra Pradesh Nritya Academy. Nataraja Rama Krishna, the President of Andhra Pradesh Nritya Academy honoured her with the membership in the Academy.

Some Chindu women were involved in prostitution in the olden days and were entertaining their patrons in the villages. Such Chindu women were married to a sword or an idol and left free for their purpose who are known as *Bhavanis*. The Children of such *Bhavanis* belonged to the mother.

In the performance of Chindus, the Ellamma role is very important. For this role they select one unmarried girl from their family. She is called *Adipapa* or *Jogitha*. They treat her as a pious one though she enjoys sexual freedom. After the completion of their performance, she goes to every house for taking donations. She agrees to have sex with the man, who is prepared to pay liberally[85]. This practice is still known as *Jogini* or *Jogita* system. The girls, after their dedication, take openly to prostitution and incur no social disgrace on that account[86].

On the last day, after the completion of their performance Chindus sacrifice a sheep near the house of the head Madiga. Later the Ellamma goes to each and every house in the village for collections.

They are all Saivites and follow Saiva traditions in their day to day life. They have *Kulapanchayats*, Voli marriage system, and widow re-marriages. They follow all the traditions and rituals of their patron-community.

Sumup

Each major community has one exclusive nomadic tribe depending on them for livelihood. In some cases, there are more than one namadic tribes attached to some major communities. These nomadic tribes will be visiting their exclusive *Mirasi* villages once in two or three years. They entertain their host communities with either stage performance or by singing the ballads exhibiting the Patams. This chapter makes an attempt to describe those entertaining folks which make use of an open-air stage for their performance and use many musical instruments in their recitation. Each tribe has its own set of orchestra, literature, and subject. Thus, there is a rich variety of cultural exuberancy represented in the variety of art forms.

These tribes, apart from their art and culture lead a disciplined social life respecting the time honoured regulations of their community. Their culture has moulded them with an unbroken tradition of various customs. Their host communities also respect their commitment to these nomadic tribes which approch them at regular intervals. Despite the fact that they are poor, they do not accept support from any other community. These nomadic tribes honestly serve their major communities by preserving their gene alogies, ***gotras***, and the legends relating to the origin of their castes.

References

1. The list of nomadic tribes attached to each major caste is given in Appendix - I.

2. **Kreedabhiramamu** mentions the existence of various castes namely Brahmins, Purohithas, Komatis, Balijas, Reddys, Kammas, Velamas, Kapus, Devangas, Carpenters, Potters, Periyas Gollas, Washermen, Barbers, Kirathas Boyas, Charmakaras, Mathangas, Thalaris, Medharas, Bestas, Jakkulas, Sangaris, Ontelas, Viramustis and Vipravinodis. Besides these we find village protectors, dental workers, poets, singers sculptures, painters, stage actors, Palnati Kathakulu, Gangireddula vandlu, Bhavanis, Asadhulu, Kolupula vandlu (tellers of puranic tales) etc.
   Vallabharayudu. Vinukonda , **Kreedhabhiramamu,** (Telugu), as quoted from N. Yadagiri Sharma, Janapada Bikshaka Gayakulu, un published Doctoral thesis, Osmania University, Hyderabad, 1986, pp. 369-370.
3. From the inscriptions of Konidesa, Penukonda, Kolanpaka, Alampuram, Warangal, Malkapuram, Pillalamarri, Durgi, Mukhtal, Nellore, Podili, Tirupati, Boorugugadda, Mudharam, Tripurantakam, Pushpagiri and also Vijayanagara inscriptions, we get information about these nomadic tribes. We also find information regarding folk arts in the ancient Sanskrit literature and in Telugu literature like-**Kreedabhiramamu, Panditharadya Charitra, Pratapa Charitam, Basava Puranam, Kumara Sambhavam, Sivathathvasaramu** and Ketana's **Dashakumara Charitra, Shimhasana Dathrimshaka, Vikrama Charitha** etc.
   Yadagiri Sharma. N, *op.cit.*, p. 371.
   Narayanamatya Ayyalaraju in his **Hamsavimsati** mentions about nomadic tribes while describing the festivities at the fair in the nineth day story. He describes various castes, customs, and professions of the Telugus in the story.
   Naranayanamatya. Ayyalaraju, **Hamsavimsati,** (Telugu), Hyderabad, 1977, p. 124.
4. Rama Raju.B, **Telugu Janapada Geya Sahityam,** (Telugu), Hyderabad, 1978, p. 9.
5. Rangacharyulu, C., Andhra Sabda Ratnakaram, Eluru, 1984, p. 1762.
   Venkata Kodananda Rao, Vishakhapatnam Zilla Vrathantam (Telugu), Vijayanagaram, 1883, p. 109.

6. Thurston, E., Castes and Tribes of Southern India, Vol. VII, Delhi, 1975, p. 406.
7. Gurubrahma sharma. G. **Kondaveeti Samrajyam** (Telugu), Guntur, 1920, pp. 21, 22.

   It is told that the Jain and the Brahmin scholars entered into a serious debate on the religious matters in the court of a king by name Sudhanya. Since they could not settle their score satisfactorily, they agreed to clinch the issue on the basis of a test of their faith in their respective religions. The Jains put a snake in a pot and sealed it. The Brahmin scholars were asked to find out what it was inside the pot. The Brahmins were perplexed and excused to reveal it by the following day. Meanwhile, they prayed Lord Surya to come to their rescue. The Lord assured them help in the court. When the court reassembled the following day, one boy came forward from the Brahmin group and declared that an icon of Lord Vishnu could be found in the pot which came out to be true on verification. The boy came to the rescue of the Brahmins and pleased them. So, the boy and his progeny have come to be known as Vipravinodis.

   Yadagiri Sharma. N, *op.cit.*, pp. 609, 610.
8. Thurston.E , *op.cit.*, p. 406.
9. Vijaya Bharathi, **Telugu Sahitya Koshamu** (Telugu), Hyderabad, 1980, p. 999.
10. Epigraphical Reports, 402 of 920, 970 of 1912 etc.
11. Srirama Apparao, **Telugu Nataka Vikasamu** (Telugu), Hyderabad, 1967, pp. 160, 162.
12. Radhakrishna Murthy.M, **Teluguvari Janapada Kala Rupalu** (Telugu), Hyderabad, 1992, pp. 291-292.
13. Rangacharyulu, *op.cit.*, p. 1245.
14. Siraj-Ul-Hassan. Sayed, **Castes and Tribes of H.E.H. the Nizam's dominions**, Delhi, 1920, p. 56.
15. Thurston.E , *op.cit.*, pp. 224-225.
16. Thurston, E. *op.cit.*, pp. 226-227.
17. Krishna Kumari. N, **Telugu Janapada Geya Gadhalu** (Telugu), Hyderabad, 1977, p. 225.
18. The Census reports of Madras (1871, 1891, 1901) and Mysore (1891 & 1901) as quoted from Thurston. E, *op.cit.* pp. 223-225.

19. Siraj-Ul-Hassan. Syed , *op.cit.*, p. 57
20. Narayanamatya. Ayyalaraju , *op.cit.*, p. 124.
21. Malkapura inscription of Kakatiyas in Guntur district and Kakandi temple inscription of Krishna Devaraya.
22. Viramustis represent themselves as having sprung from the drops of sweat which fell from the body of Virabhadra, when he destroyed the sacrifice of ***Daksha***. Virabhadra was created by Shiva from his ***Jheta*** (a lock of hair) which he dashed on the ground in a moment of frenzy on learning that ***Sati***, his wife and Daksha's daughter, had brunt herself in Daksha's sacrificial fire.
    Siraj-Ul-Hassan. Syed, *op. cit.*, p. 641.
23. The story is given in 5th Chapter, pp. 127-129.
24. ***Prabha*** resembles a temple spire in its form and is made with bamboo sticks. It is decorated with colourful pieces of cloth and adorned with the pictures of Gods and Goddesses and floral garlands.
25. Siraj-Ul-Hassan. Syed, *op.cit.*, p. 644.
26. ***Sthala*** means a ***Mirasi*** from son's side and ***Parasthala*** means a ***Mirasi*** from daughter's side. Personal interview with Viramusti Ramaiah, 60 years, Jangoan, Warangal district on 20-05-1998.
27. Siraj-Ul Hassan. Syed, *op. cit.*, p. 642.
28. Siraj-Ul-Hassan. Syed, *op.cit.*, pp. 642-643.
29. *Ibid.*
30. The Pichikuntlas take donations with the following song
    We don't have hands
    We don't have legs to walk
    We are blind
    And we are Pichikuntlas
    Please give us alms
    Somana. Palkurki, Panditaradya Charitra as quoted from Yadagiri Sharma. N, *op.cit.*, p. 327.
31. Rama Raju. B, *op.cit.*, p. 794.
32. Siraj-Ul-Hassan. Syed, *op.cit.*, p. 560.
33. Ramaraju. B, *op.cit.*, p. 795.
34. Ghanta, Katthi, Kodiche, Kamma, Pedhakanti, Lakumari, Gudadi, Motati, Pakanati, Siripapa, Burra, Chittepu, Golla, Telaga, Thuraga, Thogaru, Mada, Titthi etc..,

35. China Kamma, Peda Kamma and Gampa Kamma are the sub-sects of the Kamma caste. The different Pichikuntla families depend on them.
36. Sanikommu Pothuraju, a Pichikunti artist, residing at Buchi Reddy Palem, Banigandlapadu mandal of the Kammam district had ***Mirasi*** villages in Madira mandal. He recited stories for not less than 40 years. Now he is 70 years old and is not able to recite stories. He had five - sons. Among them two are reciting stories the remaining sons took to sheep raring profession. Potharaju take donations only from Peda kanti Reddies. He used to visit his ***Mirasis*** when he was healthy. Now the sons are not interested to take donations. So he permitted one, Seelamsivarama koti and Seelam Krishna to go to same villages for taking donations. Thus, the ***Mirasi*** villages are transferable from one to other when the farmer is not able to continue the traditional assignment.
37. గణనాయక శివగణ నాయక - పార్వతి వరపుత్రా గణనాయక ప్రత్యక్షం కావుమయ్యా గణనాయక - పూజింపుమలామయ్య గణనాయక మమ్ముందర్శి దయ జూడుమయ్య గణేశ - ఆహో ఓ - ఓ - ఓ -....
38. Siraj-Ul-Hassan. Syed, *op.cit.*, p. 571.
39. The etymology of the word Mandahechu (***Manda*** - means 'a flock of sheep' ***Hechu*** - means growth) and ***Manda pempu chese varu*** (the persons who help in increasing the flock of sheep).
40. These customs are very popular in the villages like Donakonda, Aavulapadu even to this day.
41. Keshavulu is a Mandahechu, 45 years old, from Ellandu village of Khamam district narrated this story on 24-03-1989.
42. Nagamallu, a Mandahechu, 50 years old, from Thorrur village, Warangal district narrated this story on 25-03-1999.
43. Bala Narasimham, 60 years old, from Chautuppal village, Nalgonda district, Narrated this story on 29-03-1999.
44. Narayanamatya. Ayyalaraju , *op. cit.*, p. 125.
45. Rama Raju. B, *op.cit.*, p. 225.
46. Siraj-Ul-Hassan. Syed, *op.cit.*, p. 208.
47. Subba Rao. T, **Katamaraju kathalu** Vol-I, Hyderabad 1976, p. CCL III.
48. Nagaiah. G, **Telugu Sahitya Samiksha**, Vol-I, Tirupati, 1985 p. 385.
49. See Appendix-II

50. Each family numbering 10 - 15 members.
51. According to a legend the Mandahechu tribe had originted from the union of a ***Sharadagallu*** woman of a ***Budigajangas***. Thus the Mandahechus have very close relationships with the ***Budigajangas***. Some Mandahechus even have the ***Gotras*** of ***Budigajangas*** like Teerpula, Jangari, Palakaya, Nimmakaya, Challavari, Basaram, Chintala, Chevula, Mekala, Gorrela, Ala, Ragi, Medi and Ura etc.
52. Personal interview with Ura Keshavulu, a Mandahechu from Ellandu village on 28-03-1999.
53. Thurston. E, *op.cit.*, p. 260.
    John. A.C. Boswell (ed), **Manual of the Nellore district in the presidency of Madras**, Madras, 1878, p. 10.
    Shastry. B.N, (ed), **Nalgonda Mandala Sarvaswamu**, Hyderabad, 1986, p. 289.
    Venkata Kodanda Rao, **Vishkapatnam Zilla Vruthantham**, Vijaya Nagaram 1883. p. 110.
    Sita Rama Charyulu. B, **Sabda Ratnakaramu**, Chennapatnam, 1969, p. 667.
54. Subba Chary. P., Janapada Vignanam lo Asrita Sahityam, Unpublished Doctoral Thesis, Osmania University, Hyderabad, 1992, p. 87.
55. Yadagiri sharma. N , op.cit., p. 281.
56. Jayanthi Ramaiah Panthulu, **Sri Surya Rayandra Nighantuvu**, Vol. VI, Hyderabad, 1982, p. 705.
57. Adibatla Venkataramana, **Andhra Jyothi Weekly**, dated 08-10-1982, p. 61.
58. Narayanamatya. Ayyala Raju, *op. cit.*, p. 124.
59. Yadagiri Sharma. N, *op.cit.*, p. 282.
60. Radha Krishna Murthy. M , **Teluguvari Janapada Kala Rupalu**, Hyderabad, 1992, pp. 565-566.
61. Pratapa Reddy Suravaram, **Andhrula Sangeeka Chartitra**, Hyderabad, 1992, p. 26.
62. Subba Chary. P, *op. cit.*, p. 88.
63. Census of India 1891& 1931 General Tables British provinces and feudatory states. Vol-II and Madras Presidency Vol-XV - caste Index.

64. కంచి కామాక్షికానవే
పార్వతీ కల్యాణము వినగ రారే
వర గౌరీ కల్యాణము
కంచి కామకోటి కామాక్షి...........

65.
ఎవరీ జగము లెల్ల సృజయించెను
ఎవరికైనా వివరింపంగ వశమా ॥ ఎవరీ ॥
ఖ్యాతిగ ఎనుబది నాలుగు లక్షలా – జీవకోటికి
ఆధారం బెనరే ర్వరబెదూ ॥ ఎవరీ ॥
భవుడో, మరి శ్రీధవుడో, పద్మభువుడో మరి ఎవరో
అవి రళముగ ఈ చరా చర జాలము ॥ ఎవరీ ॥
కాలానలా భీల శూలంబు నిర్మించి
శంభున కిచ్చిన శాంత మూర్తి
విక్రమ పరాక్రమం విమలైక చక్రంబు
వినుని కోసగిన విములమూర్తి
పృథివని సృష్టించి ఇలలో బ్రహ్మకుని
ఘంటంబు నిచ్చిన ఘనుడ నీవే
ఘన గిడుల్ బెకిలింప ఘనత వజ్రంబునే
దేవేంద్రుకిచ్చిన దియ్య మూర్తి
ఉన్న చోటున నీవు కన్యను సృష్టించి
భానుని కొసగిన, పరమగురువు
విమల గుణ ధర్మ ఘన మేఘ వాహనాంక
విజయ సధర్మ శ్రీవిరాట్ విశ్వకర్మ ....

66. Pasham Somasekher, a Runza artist had ***Mirasi*** rights in the villages of Krishna, Guntoor and Khammam districts. His brother Lokanatham had ***Mirasis*** in some localities of Hyderabad, Secundrabad and Rangareddy districts. Pasham Somashekar refused to give his performance in Hyderabad when the people asked him, because the Hyderabad area is under his brother Lokanadham's possession. Andhra Pradesh Government felicitated Palalochana, a Runza artist during the festival of ***Ugadi*** in Ravindra Bharathi. He had ***Mirasi*** villages in the West Godavari, East Godavari and Khammam districts. He was asked by

organisors when he was in Hyderabad to perform his art. But he refused it because the Hyderabad was not in his ***Mirasi*** village. Thus, they do not enter into other ***Mirasi*** villages.

67. Yadagiri Sharma.N , *op.cit.*, p. 285.
68. Thurston.E , *op.cit.*, p. 42.
69. Subba Chary. P , *op. cit.*, p. 88.
70. Census of India, 1891, part II, H.E.H. the Nizam's dominions, Vol.XXIII A, and caste index.
71. Thurston. E , *op.cit.*, p. 261.
72. Pentaiah, a Padmasali, 60 years old, from Hanamkonda narrated this story on 10-09-1998.
73. Parvatalu, a Sadanasurudu, 60 years old, Valbapoor village, Huzurabad Mandal, Karimnagar district, narrated this story on 18-09-1998.

    Raj Mohammad. M.D, Indrajala Pradarshakulu - Sadanasurulu, (Telugu), **Musi** monthly, July 1999, pp. 7-9.
74. Yadagiri Sharma, N., *op. cit.*, p. 454.
75. Pandavula Ramulu, 50 years old, Secundrabad, narrated this story on 16-12-1998.
76. Personal interview with Pandavula Manikyam, 70 years old, Attapuram, Ranga Reddy district, on 20-12-1998.
77. Reddy G.N, Mandalika Vrithipadakosam, Vol. V. ***Kummaram***, Hyderabad, 1976, p. 11.
78. Subba Chary. P, *op.cit.*, p. 116.
79. Paidipala Agaiah, a Potter, 70 years old, Hanamkonda, Warangal district, narrated this story on 19-08-1998.
80. Siraj-Ul-Hassan. Sayed, *op.cit.*, p. 412.
81. ***Yakshaganam*** is a theatrical performing folk art form wherein music, dance, speech and make-up (costume) - all the four arts are harmoniously blended into one. This is common to Karnataka also. The earliest reference to it is found in Palkuriki Somanatha's ***Panditharadhya Charitra*** and the oldest ***Yakshaganas*** available in Telugu belong to 15th and 16th centuries. The name ***Yakshaganam*** suggests that it was recitation of ***desi*** music by a ***Yaksha*** or ***Yakshini*** in its earlier state and after some time evolved into narration of episodes with the aid of more than one character and finally developed into opera with different kinds of songs, dialogues and numerous characters. ***Yakshas*** are mentioned

as celestials along with ***Garudas, Ghandharvas*** and ***Kinneras*** in our ancient lore.

The early ***Yakshagana*** contain ***desi*** compositions like ***Daruvu, Ragada, Jampe, Dwipada, Ela, Sobhanam, Davalam, Mangalarathi*** besides ***Sandi vacanam*** - small link words in prose which developed into dialogues lateron. Later ***Yakshaganas*** developed many nuances and adopted some of the features of classical Sanskrit drama.

The themes of ***Yakshagana*** plays of earlier centuries were drawn mainly from the ***Ramayana***, the ***Mahabharatha***, the ***Bagavatha*** and other ***Puranas***. Lateron contemporary historical, social and political themes were also enacted.

Rama Raju. B , ***Glimpses in to Telugu folklore***, Hyderabad, 1991, pp. 87-88.

82. *Ibid.*
83. Radhakrishna Murthy. M , op.cit. p. 369.
84. In the Armoor troupe, along with Chindula Ellamma, Chindula Srinivas, Chindula Venkataratnam, Chindula Rajeshwar, Chindula Balaiah, Chindula Neelamma, Susheela are the important artists. In the story of ***Sarangadhara***, they perform different roles and got a special place among all the Chindu troupes belonged to Andhra Pradesh. In the play of ***Sarangadhara***, Chindula Shyam plays as Raja Raja Narendra, Chindula Srinivas as ***Sarangadhara***. Chindula Ellamma as Chitrangi and Chindula Rajeshwar as Chelikatthe. In this troupe Chindula Gopal plays on ***Maddela***, Srimathi on cybols, Chandraiah on Harmoniam.
85. Lalitha, op.cit., p. 102.
86. Syed Siraj-Ul-Hassan, op.cit., p. 412.

4

Art and Culture of Patapradarshana Kathakulu

While some nomadic tribes give stage performances to entertain their patron communities, some other tribes use descriptive and pictorial maps known as *Patams,* charts, figures, idols, terracotta figures in their narrations of stories, genealogies etc. This chapter describes the life and culture of such tribes who are known as *Patapradarshanakathakulu.* The *Patams* usually are about thirty yards long and one yard wide. This *Patam* (cloth) is wound to a stick. They plant two sticks of 'Y' shape and put on the encircled *Patam* when they start reciting the stories. They pull the *Patam* slowly like a film reel and show the pictures and narrate the story accordingly. They hang these *Patams* on the dais and the main singer of the troupe explains it with a pointer while they recite the stories to their patron-communities. The main singer holds a pointer of one yard or half yard long with a silver knob at the end. He shows the figures on the *Patam* with this pointer and tells the story. He recites the story in the method of *Yakshagana*. The narration includes poetry, prose and songs. The main singer is supported by two other singers called *Vanthalu* with musical instruments. The *Patams* are prepared by the people of *Nakasi* caste in multi colours to all the dependant castes of various communities, according to their requirements. The cost of each *Patam* ranges between Rs. 500 and Rs. 3000.

Padmasali Community

Kunapulivaru

Kunapulivaru take donations from Padmasali community by reciting *Padma puranam* or *Bhavana Rishi Mahatyam* once in three years[1]. They are also called *Padigerajulu*[2], *Padigidderajulu, Sainollu* and *Pulijendavaru* in Andhra Pradesh. By profession they are all mendicants belonging to Padmasali community, but they are called by different names in different regions of Andhra Pradesh. They make a living by leading nomadic life depending on the Padmasali community.

The origin of Kunapulivaru and the lineage of Padmasalis are described in the *Bhavana Rishi Mahatyam.* According to it Bhavana Rishi was the founder of Padmasali community. He waged a war against giant Kaluva. In this war Kunapuli army fought in support of Bhavana Rishi. With the help of Kunapuli army Bhavana Rishi killed giant Kaluva in the battle. Then Bhavana Rishi recognised the services renderd by Kunapuli army in the war and bestowed a boon on them to get support for their livelihood from Padmasali community by reciting *Bhavana Rishi Mahatyam.* From then onwards, they became a dependant caste of Padmasalis[3].

Kunapulivaru tour villages along with a flag called *Pulijenda* and plant it in front of the house of the head Padmasali (*Kulapedda*), to announce their arrival. Later, they go from house to house with their musical instruments, bless them and return to the house of head Padmasali. The same night they recite stories for Padmasali community. They start with a prayer to Ganapathi, Saraswathi, Brahma, Vishnu, Siva, Markandeya and Bhavana Rishi before starting the stories. They mainly recite the *Markandeyacharitra* and *Bhavana Rishi Mahatyam.*

After the completion of the stories, Kunapulivaru visit the Padmasali houses and bless the inmates with chants. Before blessing their hosts they first recite a poem. Then they wish their hosts the best of health, wealth and happiness. They preach some important maxims emphasizing the need for the neatness, vegetarianism, non-alcoholism[4] etc. Later, they take contributions from Padmasalis which is called *Tyagam* and go to another village. They have their own *Mirasi* villages in Andhra Pradesh. Thus, they lead a nomadic life.

They are all Saivites. They follow Saivite tradition in their day-to-day life. We find the Kunapuli families in Mangalagiri (Guntoor), Nellore, Cuddapah, Tadipatri, Bellary (Karnataka), Jagityal, Huzurabad (Karimnagar dist.) and Bayyaram, Mahaboobabad, Chintagattu, Pattipaka, Sayampeta (Warangal dist.) areas. Now their art is declining due to the lack of patronisation from their hosts. As a result they are all practicing different professions for their livelihood. For instance, the Kunapulis of Sayampeta are engaged in textile business and in Chintagattu, they have turned to weaving.

Mutrasi Community

Kakipadigelavaru

Kakipadigelavaru[5] take donations from Mutrasi or Mudiraj community only[6] once in two or three years. They are also called as *Kakirekkalavaru* and *Kakipadigollu*. They recite the genealogies and *Gotras* of Mutrasi community. Even both Pandavulavaru and Kakipadigelavaru depend on Mutrasi community for their livelihood but they have their respective *Mirasi* villages for taking donations in Andhra Pradesh.

Several meanings are offered like flag, pillar, and sign to the word of *Padige*[7]. The word *Padige* was mentioned in Telugu literary works, particularly in *Eddemmakatha*[8], and *Matha Puranam*[9]. They go with a flag or a staff with a metal crow to their patron-community. They plant *Kaki dhwajam* (a flag) in front of the dais and start telling story with the help of *Patam*. They tell the origin and evolution of Mutrasi community. If any family of their patron community refuses to pay to them, they throw a dead crow on their house which means a curse. The Mutrasis generally do not refuse to pay their contribution.

There is a legend regarding the origin of the Kakipadigelavaru. According to it in olden days the Kakipadigelas belonged to Mutrasi community. Their main profession was collecting the fruits from forest which they claimed a monopolistic right and to sell them to the people in towns and villages for their livelihood. The Mutrasi monopoly of forest fruit trees is called *Penthotavanam*. Once upon a time, a Mutrasi killed a crow, which was pecking a fruit in *Penthotavanam*. Then *Penthota peddamma* the *Shakti* Goddess, cursed[10] him to beg from Mutrasi community exhibiting a crow flag. From then onwards his descendants came to be known as Kakipadigelavaru[11].

Siraj-Ul-Hassan recorded another legend regarding the origin of *Kakipadigelavaru*. According to that during the times of *Ramayana* one tribal lady known as Sabari (also known as Mutrasi tribal) woman was collecting the fruits from forest and selling them in the near by town which was their traditional occupation. One day when she was selling the fruit in the streets, she was called by a Panchadayi house-wife who bought one fruit and gave it to her child. While the house-wife was settling the price, the child ate a bit of the fruit and threw it into the fruit basket by which all the fruits were deemed to have been contaminated. Sabari woman demanded the cost of the damage from the Panchadayi woman and abused her. The house-wife was angry about it and sent a big iron mass like a crow to destroy Sabari's fruit grove. The crow damaged the grove but it was attacked and wounded by the second son of Sabari before, crow could escape from the scene. Sabari's second son pursued it further and could not return to his house for about two months and by that time Sabari felt that he was dead and performed the last rites for him. After some time he returned home, the Mutrasi community did not accept him in to their fold as he touched the crow, which was considered as a condemnable act. Therefore, he was ex communicated. His descendants came to be known as Kakipadigelavaru[12].

Kakipadigelas exhibit a *Patam* during their performance while narrating stories. The *Patam* consists of relevant pictures of gods, goddesses, heroes of Mutrasi community etc., in multi colours.

These pictures are action pictures and show the dress, ornaments, weapons etc., of those times and give a continuous theme of the events and preserve their heritage and culture.

The *Kulapedda* (head of Mutrasi caste) fixes the day for the performance for Mutrasi community. The main singer wears white *Shirt*, *Dhoti*, red colour head dress (*paga*) and holds a pointer in his right hand to show the pictures related to the story on *Patam*. He wears *Gajjalu* (anklets or gridle of small bells) on his ankles. The supporting singers will help in reciting the story with their musical instruments like *maddela* and *Harmonium*. They start the main story with a long prayer songs devoted to Goddess Sharada[13], Ganapathi[14], Goddess Durga and *Penthota peddamma*.

They recite the stories regarding the origin and evolution of Mutrasi community like *Pandavavanavasamu*, *Virataparvamu*, *Drawpadi Vastrapaharanamu* etc., on the request of the host community. On the last day of their performance the entire Mutrasi community celebrates the *Bonalu* festival to the Goddess *Penthota Peddamma* and give donations to the Kakipadigelavaru.

They get about Rs. 500/- for each visit and new clothes from Mutrasi community of the village. Thus, they tour all their *Mirasi* villages once in two or three years. They have a language of their own which has no script. We find them in Khammam, Karimnagar, Medak and Warangal districts. We find considerable number of these families in the villages of Narmetta, Bachannapeta, Cherial of Warangal district.

Rajaka Community

Rajaka community has two dependant sub-castes, namely Patamuvaru and Ganjikutivaru.

(i) Patamuvaru

Patamuvaru take donations from Rajaka community (washer men) only. They are also called Patamollu, Patamchakallu or Arogya Brahmins in Andhra Pradesh. They recite Rajaka Puranam which is also called Basavapuranam or Basava Vijayamu with the help of a *Patam* in which they trace the origin and evolution of the *Rajaka* community.

There is a legend regarding the origin of Patamuvaru. According to it, Virabhadra who was sent to destroy *Daksha Yajna* by Lord Siva, was supposed to have committed a grave sin by the destruction of *Yajna* which was equal to that of killing of gods. Siva though admired Virabhadra for his valour and achievement, ordered him to wash the clothes of gods to propitiate his sin. Virabhadra went to *Swarnakamala sarasu* and he was very much disturbed how to do this job. While he was worrying about the ignominy of such act, two drops of his sweat fell on two *Kamalams* (lotus flowers) in the lake. One such drop emerged as Madivelu Machaiah who was ordered to wash the clothes of gods. After completing the job, he approached Virabhadra and prayed him to show him the source for his livelihood. Virabhadra asked him to go to *Bhuloka* and wash the clothes of men and thus earn his livelihood. His progeny came to be known as Rajakas. Another person who emerged out of the drop of sweat of Virabhdra from another lotus flower refused to wash the clothes. He was cursed by Virabhadra to depend on the Rajakas for the livelihood. Thus a dependant caste of Patamuvaru came into being[15].

The story of Madivelu Machaiah is also described in *Basavapuranam*[16]. We also find *Machaiah katha* in the folk songs of Karnataka[17]. The Rajakas worship Madivelu Machaiah as an incarnation of Virabhadra.

Patamuvaru visit their *Mirasi* villages once in three years to recite *Rajaka Puranam* and *Gotras* of Rajakas. In the *Rajaka Puranam* they narrate *Madivelu Machaiah's* origin, family and the war between *Madivelu Machaiah* and *Bijjala Raju* etc.

Their art form is also called *Patapradarshana Katha* because they exhibit the *Patam*. In this *Patam* each phase of the story is illustrated in a frame of 2 ft. long. Like wise the entire main aspects of *Rajaka Puranam* are printed. They coil this *Patam* to a stick and preserve it in a box made of either iron or bronze.

At the beginning and also at the end of the performance they usually offer a coconut to the *Patam*. They worship *Patam* with utmost devotion. They put turmeric and *kumkum* on the box in which they preserve it. They place *Patam* near the idols of the gods in the home and treat it as sacred. When the *patam* becomes fragile after the passage of time, they perform the death rituals to it and discord it. *Induluri Munnuswamy*, a *Patam* artist explained regarding his *Patam* that it is 100 years old. It was given to his father by his grand father, later, he inherited it from his father. In this *Patam* some parts are in brittled condition and he covered it by pasting another cloth to its back. Thus, they pay sincere attention to the preservation of the *Patam*.

They start the story with the prayer to Goddess *Sharada,* Lord *Ganapathi* and *Madivelu Machaiah*. The team mainly consists of three artists. The main singer recite the story in prose, songs and *Slokas* by showing *Patam* with a pointer. He wears *Dhoti*, shirt and turban. They are Saivites and also wear *jandyam, lingas*, and a chain of *rudraksha*. Two supporting singers sit on either side of the main singer on dais. Their dresses are similar to that of main singer. One plays on *Maddela*, another on cybols when main singer recite the story. Along with these members, three to four other members also sit at the back side of the dais, and join the chorus during the performance who are amateurs.

In the recent times, the *Rajakas* are not able to enjoy the *Patapradarshana Katha* of the *Patamuvaru*. How ever, the troupe members of this *Patamuvaru* are visiting the houses of their patron-community in the districts of Telangana and Rayalaseema and take donations from them by merely showing the *Patams*.

We find Patamuvaru in Sathupalli, Bethupalli in Khammam district, Ganapuram, Mulugu, Vardhannapeta, Bollikunta, Manukota in Warangal district, Peddapalli, Manthini in Karimnagar district, Kodada, Buvanagiri, Armoor in Nalgonda district, Rayapadu, Khambam in Prakasham district and in some parts of Nellore district of Andhra Pradesh.

(ii) Ganjikutivaru

Ganjikutivaru also depend on *Rajakas*. Gangikutivaru and Patamuvaru are two different sub-castes. They do not have matrimonial relations between them. They are found in Sathupalli and Bethupalli of Khammam district and they have their own *Mirasi* villages. They claim that they are *Arogya Brahmins*[18].

There is a legend regarding the origin of Ganjikutivaru. According to it Madivelu Machaiah the founder of Rajaka community as a Saivite had taken an oath that he would not wash the clothes of non-Saivites. During that time a non-Saivite king by name Bijjala Raju was ruling. Madivelu Machaiah and his community refused to wash the clothes of the Raja. One Rajaka disobeyed Madivelu Machaiah and washed the clothes of the Raja. So Madivelu Machaiah ex-communicated him. When he again prayed for his livelihood, Madivelu Machaiah allowed him to depend on his community. His progeny in course of time were called Ganjikutivaru[19].

They also recite *Rajaka puranam* in which they trace the origin and evolution of Rajakas. They visit Rajakas once in three years. Their art performance and content of the recital are not different from that of Patamuvaru. We also find them in Rajahmundry, Guntur, Prakasham and Telangana districts of Andhra Pradesh.

Gouda Community

Gouda community aslo has two dependant sub-castes namely (i) Goudajettis, (ii) Enutivaru.

(i) Goudajettis

Goudajettis take donations only from Gouda community in Andhra Pradesh. They are also called *Jettollu* and *Shettis*. In the *Suryarayandhra Nigantuvu*, the meaning of the word 'Gouda' is mentioned as the seller of toddy[20]. There is also another meaning for the word Gouda i.e. a village head[21]. The people who draw toddy from Palm tree and Date Palm tree are called Goudas in Andhra Pradesh. They are also called *Ediga*. The word *Ediga* is very popular in Rayalaseema. Goudajettis take donations from Gouda and Ediga castes only by reciting *Goudapuranam* in which they narrate the origin and evolution of the Gouda community. Besides *Goudapuranam* they also recite *Katamaiahkatha, Surabhandeshwarakatha* in which they explain their origin and their dependance on Gouda community.

The Census reports of the Nizam State and the Madras Presidency, did not mention the existence of this caste, because they considered themselves belonging to Gouda community. But infact, they are a dependant caste of Goudas.

There is a legend regarding the origin of the Goudajettis, which was mentioned in *Goudapuranam*. Sage Koundinya was born to Brahma. He had five sons and one daughter with the blessings of Brahma. They were Adi Gouda, Amara Gouda, Veda Gouda, Viprama Gouda, Pungama Gouda and Chellamadevi. Challamadevi was married to Katamaiah. They were all collectively working for their livelihood. Adi Gouda was producing toddy from Palm tree. Amara Gouda was producing toddy from Date Palm tree. The other brothers, sister and her husband were selling toddy at *Manduva* (toddy-shop). In those times PungamaGouda and Katamaiah both were jointly donating a portion of their profit in the name of Lord Siva. Adi Gouda, Amara Gouda and Veda Gouda did not approve of this and left for another place. But they lost all of their property and forts and were ex-communicated from their caste by Katamaiah. Again on their request, they were allowed to depend on the Goudas for their livelihood. Since then they are called Goudajettis. One of the sections of this community (Veda Gouda) who left for a distant place by crossing a stream. Later, they were called Enutivaru (*Erudatinavaru*), since they crossed the stream[22]. Thus, the Goudajettis and Enutivaru became dependant sub-castes of Goudas.

There is another legend[23] regarding the origin of Goudajettis. According to it the *Pancha Goudas* (Adigouda, Amaragouda, Vedagouda, Vipramagouda, Pungamagouda), who were irresponsible towards their profession, and were neglecting their duties were cursed by Lord Siva and as a result Adi Gouda became hunter, Amara Gouda became Goudajetti, Veda Gouda became Edigavadu,

VipramaGouda became the protector of *Koundinya Gotra* and Pungama Gouda became the priest. Thus, according to that legend the second one, Amara Gouda became Goudajetti who recite the stories to Goudas.

Goudajettis visit Gouda community for taking donations once in two years. They recites the *Goudapuranam* and *Surabhandeshwarakatha* by exhibiting a *Patam* related to *Goudapuranam.* The pictures of Katamaiah[24] as he was riding a horse in the Palm tree grove and pictures of Ellamma and Mysamma adjacent to Katamaiah appear in the *Patam* at the time of their performance.

The *Patam* also consists of pictures of Rishi Koundinya, Brahma, Shiva, Vayu, Narada, Parvathi, Suramambha, Challamamba, the Palm trees, the *Panchagoudas* and the tools related to the Gouda profession. The following tools related to Gouda profession are also printed in *Patam*.

1. **Musthadu** : It is a belt, in which the knife and other weapons are placed, which are useful for drawing the toddy from tree.

2. **Mokhu** : It is a ring wich is used to climb the Palm tree.

3. **Gutthi** : It is another ring which is also used to climb the tree.

4. **Katthi** : It is a knife which is used to draw the toddy.

5. **Karugola** : It is an instrument to sharpen the knives.

6. **Lotti** : It is a small pot used to collect toddy from the tree.

There are two methods in the recitation of Goudajettis. One is *Patamkatha*, in which they recite *Goudapuranam* by showing the

Patam. The other one is called *Bhagavatha* method in which they makeup themselves as different characters and recite the *Goudapuranam* with action, song and dance as in a drama. They perform either *Patamkatha* or *Bhagavatha* or both as desired by the hosts. Generally the Goudajetti troupe consists of five members in the *Patamkatha*. The main singer usually wears a white shirt, *Dhoti* and turban and holds a pointer to show the pictures related to the story on the *Patam*. The supporting singers also wear similar dress. They recite the story regularly for five days in each village. Before the commencement of the story, they pray Goddess Saraswathi, Ganapathi, Siva, Parvathi, Vishnu and later, Katamaiah and their caste goddesses. The style of their recitation is simple and easily understandable even to illiterate men, women and children.

After the completion of the story telling, on the last day, the Goudas celebrate the *Bonalu* festival to their God Katamaiah. During this festival the Goudajettis draw *muggu* (Rangoli) with five colours which is called *Patnam* in Telugu. In the middle of the *muggu* they place the *Bonam* (pot) which is coated with turmeric and *kumkum*. Later, they serve the cooked food from *Bonam* in different banyan leaves and offer to their Goddess along with a sheep sacrifice. Then they mix food with sheep blood and sprinkle it on their houses and on professional tools and pray for the well-being of their families. After this festival Goudajetties collect their donations (*thyagam*) from Goudas and go to another village. Thus, they collect a sheep, some grain and about Rs. 500 to 3000 in their visit to a village once in two years.

Goudajettis follow Saiva tradition, and wear *lingas* around their neck. They follow different systems of marriage, one of them is *Voli*. The practices like widow re-marriage, divorce, child marriages and re-marriage of divorcee etc., are in vogue. *Kulapanchayats* are being practiced in their caste. They celebrate all the Hindu festivals such as Deepavali, Dasara, Sankranthi and Ugadi etc. They also follow the traditions, customs and rituals of Gouda community, and celebrate *Bonalu* festival to Goddess Kalika and Katamaiah once in a year. They respect Jangas as their *Gurus*.

We find them in Ganapuram, Mulugu, Narsampeta, Thorrur, Mahaboobabad, Jangoan, of Warangal district ; Anantharam, Buvanagiri of Nalgonda district and Rajahmundry in East Godavari district. They are also found in Guntoor, East Godavari and Karimnagar districts.

(ii) Enutivaru

Enutivaru also depend on Goudas. Goudajettis mainly recite the stories by showing exhibits i.e. the *Patam*, but *Enutivaru* mainly recite the *Gotras* without any exhibits.

The *Gotras* of Goudas are well preserved by Enutivaru in oral form for generations together. According to them the *Gotras* of Goudas are *Koundinya, Karunya, Vatsalya, Surabhandeshwara* etc.

They are considered untouchables by the Goudas. So they are treated lower than *Goudajettis* in their social status[25].

Mangali Community

Addapollu

Addapollu depend on barber (Mangali) or *Nayibrahmins* community. They visit their *Mirasi* villages once in two years and recite a legend called *Mangali puranam* in which they present the origin and evolution of *Mangali* caste and their caste. To day, their number is very small. In olden days they used to recite the stories along with a *Patam* but at present it is not being exhibited.

In the areas of Telangana and Rayalaseema they are called Addapollu. In Guntur, Krishna, Vijayawada, Nellore, Prakasham, East Godavari, Srikakulam, Vijayanagaram and Vishakapatnam districts they are called *Addam Singas* or *Addam singarulu*[26].

There is a legend regarding the origin and evolution of the Addapu caste. Nayibrahmin (Mangali) was born from the sweat of Virabhadra. He used to stay with Lord Siva and learned music, *Nadaswara*, when Lord Siva was dancing. Then Lord Siva blessed him. This Nayibrahmin (Mangali) had two sons. One day the elder son took his food at Vishnu's place. This infuriated his father, who ex-communicated him from Nayibrahmin caste and ordered him to live by showing his palm like mirror to others indicating hair dressing profession. Thus, he became *Mangali* and the other a musician. Some of their progeny did not learn either their professional skills or music who became Addapusingas[27] to recite *Gotras* of Mangalis and to depend on them for their livelihood.

They recite stories during daytime. The Addapu troupe consists of 6 members. Cybols, Harmonium and drum called *maddela* are their musical instruments. The main singer wears white shirt, *Dothi* and turban and the supporting singers wear similar dresses. They pray goddess Saraswathi and God Ganapathi, Shiva before the commencement of the story. The style of their recitation of *Kirthanas* are called *Bhaghavatha* method. They used to recite the stories of *Dhakshayagnam*, *Parvati Kalyanam*, *Virabadrajananam*. But now they are reciting only *Gotras* of *Mangali* community. They are Saivites and follow Saivite traditions in their day-to-day life.

We find them in very small numbers in Andhra Pradesh. The only source to know about their culture is their patron-community, i.e. *Mangalis*.

Madiga Community

Dakkalis

Dakkalis take donations only from Madiga community by reciting *Jambavapuranam*, playing on *Kinnera*, a musical instrument. They are considered untouchables by the Madigas and also by their another dependant nomadic tribe Chindu Madigas. The Madigas do not even allow their wives to see the Dakkalis. Thus, they are the lowest of the low in the social status.

In Kurnool district they are said to have divided the district with the *Mustis* (groups of *Mirasi* villages) and not to beg except within their own limits[28].

"The Dakkalis are nomadic beggers, who appear to be a degraded branch of the Madigas and beg only from them. They are also the genealogists or custodians of the *gotras* of their parent caste", writes Syed Siraj-Ul-Hassan[29].

Their main profession is to recite *Jambavapuranam* in which they present the origin of their caste, and also recite the *gotras* and genealogies of Madigas. Dakkalis play *Kinnera* as a musical accompaniment to their recital.

E. Thurston recorded a legend[30] regarding the origin of the Dakkali caste. "A smith was asked to make a *Kalyana Tilakam* (An auspicious mark on forehead) for Siva's wedding and for this purpose required bellows, fire pot, hammer etc. Jambavantha killed his eldest son and prepared the various implements from sundry parts of the body, except the back bone. Being highly pleased at this, the God endowed the backbone with life and the son went to his father Jambavantha, who failed to recognise him and refused to accept him as his son. He was told that he must live as a begger attached to the Madigas and was called Dakkala because he was brought to life from vertebral column (*dakka*)".

Siraj-Ul-Hassan recorded another legend regarding the origin of Dakkali caste. "It is said that Heppu Muni, the eldest son of Jambavantha, after being killed by Brahma for the creation of worlds, was restored to life by his father, but was degraded and condemned to subsist by begging from and reciting the mythical history of the Madiga and Manga (a north Indian caste equivalent to Madigas) castes. They have heriditary rights, and if any Madiga declines to give them their due, they mount his effigy on a bamboo pole and set it up infront of his house. Standing in the neighbourhood, they hurl at him horrible imprecations and curses ; he remains under the ban of his caste and no one dares to maintain any communication with him until he thoroughly satisfies the demands of the refractory beggers. The Dakkalawads say that they have only one *Gotra Gangadhar*. They all regarded as out castes by the Madigas and are not allowed to enter their quarters, but they pitch their huts of bamboo mats at a distance from the Madiga houses"[31].

The Dakkalis wander from place to place for their livelihood. They are served food outside the houses of Madigas by only the male members as females are not allowed to see them.

The Dakkalis wear *Vibhuti* all over their body. They wear Jandyam across the shoulders and *Dhoti*. They hold a stick in the right hand and a palm-leaf manuscripts on the left hand. They have a good boisterous tone.

They recite *Jambavapuranam* and exhibit *Patam*. The most important musical instrument of them is *Kinnera*. Narayanamatya mentioned about *Kinnera*[32]. They make *Kinnera* themselves. Along with *Kinnera* they also use *maddela*, harmonium, cybols in their performance. They also recite songs about *Bondolla Kurumanna*, *Panduga Sayanna Katha*, which are known as *Kinnera patalu*.

After the completion of their performance they collect their donations from Madigas and go to other villages. Thus, they lead a nomadic life. *Dakuru, Karne, Bonalu, Renikunta, Gouramma, Anthalollu, Allamvallu, Patati, Pittala, Pinjari* are the important *Gotras* of Dakkalis of Andhra Pradesh.

They are Saivites. They celebrate all Hindu festivals. They also have a tribal like language which has no script. They are all non-vegetarians. Some of them prepare medicines for various deceases. Some recite *Panchangas* to Madigas. Every year they must celebrate Pochamma *Bonalu*. They have *KulaPanchayats*.

We find them in Khammam, Nizamabad, Nalgonda, Medak, Karimnagar and Warangal districts.

Mala Community

Gurram Vallu

They are attached to Mala community. They recite *gotras* and geneologies of Malas and depend on them for their livelihood. They are also called *Gurram malalu* in Andhra Pradesh. They are untouchables to Malas. They have *Mirasi* villages in Telangana. Gurram Malas visit their *Mirasi* villages once in two years.

They live in huts made of palm leaves on the outskirts of villages. Regarding the degradation of the Gurram Malas it is said that a member of the sub-caste was employed to return the horse which was brought for the procession in a Mala Marriage, when he came back, by that time the marriage feast was over, and he was compelled to dine of what was left[33]. Thus, his progeny became a dependant caste of Malas.

Medara Community

Adikodukulu

Adikodukulu depend on *Medara* community. They are also called as *Arthibiddalu*. They have *Mirasi* villages in Telangana. They recite the legend of Medara caste narrating their origin.

The legend says that a mat maker was required on the occasion of the weddings of the three primeval pairs, Vishnu and Laxmi, Brahma and Saraswathi and Siva and Parvathi. One was created from a clay image to prepare the mats. Thus, the Medara community was born. In course of time some of the members of Medara caste were ex-communicated from the Medara caste, due to a mistake and became a dependant caste of Medaras. In course of time they were named as Adikodukulu[34]. The only source to know about them is their patron community. Now we can hardly find them in Andhra Pradesh.

Sum up

The nomadic tribes who use pictorial charts in their narrations known as *Pata pradarshana kathakulu* who narrate the stories relating to the origin of their respective patron-community and the emergence of their own sub-castes within the major community in a sequential order. They recite the glory of their respective communities and explain the importance and place of their community in the larger context. These sub-castes who depend on their major communities have a fixed format in presenting their narrations which is mostly common to all sub-castes of this category. Their prayers which are sung before the commencement of their performance are dedicated to all important Hindu gods and goddesses and each sub-caste also say prayers to their community God or the sage who are exclusive to their major community. Their narrations are also composed in the *Dwipada Manjeera* metre and characteristically do not differ with the language and style of the mendicants belonging to the category of stage performers.

References

1. Subba Chary. P, *op.cit.*, p. 104.
   Yadagiri Sharma. N , *op.cit.*, pp. 292-298.
2. Thurston. E, *op.cit.*, p. 118.
3. Bhikshapathi, 45 years old, from Sayampet village, Warangal District narrated this storv on 17-03-1998.
4. వంశము ఋషి వంశము, ప్రొద్దుకు మూడు స్నానాలు - ఉదయం స్నానం, మధ్యాహ్న స్నానం, సాయంత్రం స్నానం, సూరాపానం ముట్టుకోరాదు, అబద్ధమాడరాదు, కోళ్ళను కోయరాదు.
5. The community carrying a crow symbol on a flag.
6. Siraj-Ul-Hassan. Syed , *op.cit.*, p. 527.
7. Yadagiri Sharma. N, *op. cit.*, p. 462.
8. పడిగెలు, గొడుగులు పల్లకిలో అరిగెలు ....
   Eddemmakatha as quoted from Yadagirisharma. N , op.cit., p. 462.
9. పట్టుకుంచెలు కదిలే - పడిగెలు గదిలె
   పట్టుకుంచెలుబాయే - పడిగెలుబాయె
   వందగంటలుబాయే - జమిడికలుబాయె
   బోడు గంటలుబాయే - బోనములుబాయె
   మాత రంధనలన్ని - మహిమీద గూలె

   Ibid.
10. కాకిని పట్టుట కారణంబున కాన
    ఇది ముది వంశమందున్న మర్యాద కాదు
    ముదిరాజు వార్కి నీవు అడ్డివై యుండి
    జీవించుపొమ్మిక ముదిరాజు కొడుకా .....
11. Kistaiah, a Kakipadigela artist, 75 years old, Warangal district, narrated this story on 17-08-1998.
12. Siraj-Ul-Hassan. Syed, *op.cit.*, pp. 527, 528.
13. శారదాంబా ఇందూ ప్రభావే
    సకల లోకా వందాన - నరగూన బ్రోవవే ॥ శారదాంబా ॥
    నీలవేణి నిన్ను మదిలోన నమ్మ్మాతి
    కలహంస వాహనా కరుణా జూడవే మమ్మ్మా ॥ శారదాంబా ॥

14. విఘ్నాల దొలగించే వెంకయ్య నిను గొల్తు
    మూషిక వాహనా - మునిజన వంద్యూడా ॥ విఘ్నాల ॥
    ఏనుగూ తొండామూ - ఏకదంతామూ
    మోదొక హస్తాము - ముదిమార గొలిచేదా ॥ విఘ్నాల ॥

    Personal interview with Kistaiah, a Kakipadigela artist, from Warangal district on 17-08-1998.

15. Induri Kotaiah, 63 years old, Ganapuram village, Mulugu, Warangal district, narrated this story on 19-5-1997.

16. Susheela devi T, **Andhra Dwipada Sahitya Charitra**, Hyderabad, 1979, p. 56.

17. Yadagirisharma. N, *op.cit.*, p. 325.

18. Personal interview with Thurai Rajalingam, 70 years old, from Mulugu village, Warangal district on 24-1-1999.

19. Induru Gurumurthy, Ramappa village, Mulugu Mandal, Warangal district narrated this story on 20-06-1998.

20. Jayanthi Ramaiah Panthulu, **Suryarayandhra Niganttuvu**, *op. cit.*, p. 876.

21. Satya Narayana. K , **Andhrula Charitra - Samskruthi**, Vol. II, Hyderabad, 1982, p. 22.

22. Akula Venkataiah, a Goudajetti artist, 60 years old, Mulugu village, Warangal distrcit, narrated this story on 19-08-1998.

23. Yadagiri Sharma. N, *op.cit.*, p. 302.

24. The Goudas believe that the Katamaiah is an incarnation of Lord Siva. Goudajettis recite about him in ***Surabhandeshwarakatha***. The Goudas celebrate ***Bonalu*** festival on the name of Katamaiah, every year in the Palm groves. Katamaiah is said to be the God of Palm trees.

25. Personal interview with Venkataiah, a Gouda, 60 years old, Gundla Singaram village, Warangal district on 19-08-1998.

26. Personal interview with Addanki Sambasiva Rao, Secretary, Nayibrahmin Society, Andhra Pradesh, Guntur district on 19-08-1998.

27. Personal interview with Venkatesham, Addapu caste, Medichal, Ranga Reddy district, on 18-09-1998.

28. Thurston. E , *op.cit.*, pp. 104 - 105.
29. Siraj-Ul-Hassan. Syed, *op.cit.*, p. 413.
30. Thurston. E, *op.cit.*, pp. 104 - 105.
31. Siraj-Ul-Hassan. Syed, *op.cit.*, p. 413.
32. Ayyala Raju Narayana Matya, *op.cit.*, p. 124.
33. Siraj-Ul-Hassan. Syed, *op.cit.*, p. 430.
34. Sivaiah, 65 years old, Hanamkonda, Warangal district narrated this story on 19-5-1999.

5

Orality and Historicity

The nomadic tribes mainly deal with the stories related to their patron-community in Andhra Pradesh. They also keep the family history and pedigree of their host community. These stories are transmitted from one generation to the other in oral form. Later, during the medieval period the stories were composed in *Dwipada Manjeera* metre by a number of poets. Some of the copies are preserved in Madras Oriental Manuscript Library and Sri Venkateshwara Oriental Manuscript Library. Each group of a nomadic tribe keeps a copy of the manuscript of the stories, irrespective of the fact, whether they are literates are not.

The nomadic tribes also exhibit *Patam,* when they recite the stories to their patron community in which the entire story or *Purana* is printed in the form of pictures. The tribes and host communities treat the *puranas* as sacred. The nomadic tribes recite different stories in which they trace the origin of their patron caste and also their sub-caste. They narrate life-stories of the historical personalities of thier host community. The content of such narrations may be classified as,

(A) Puranic Legends and

(B) Historical Events

A. Puranic Legends

The puranic legends as narrated by these tribes reveal the origin of thier patron community and also their own sub-caste. In the process of tracing their origin, they link themselves up with a legend from *Purana.* This enables them to claim a respectable status in the society. In their further narrations, they describe a historical event particularly belonging to the medieval times in which their community takes pride in the narration. This chapter presents the *Puranic* and the historical content of their narrations. An attempt is also made to place the historical events in a proper setting of historical time-frame.

Most of the nomadic tribes recite the caste myths of their patron-community known as *Kula Puranas.* They are narrated by nomadic tribes for a specific purpose[1]. Levistraus, Cluad termed these *Puranic* accounts as legends[2]. These legends narrated by nomadic tribes ascribe a respectable social status and a distinguishable identity to their patron-communities. The patrons staunchly believe these legends which give them a clear picture of their traditions, rituals and the morals originating from their unknown past. These legends form the basis for reconstructing the history of the evolution of castes and the communities.

Pichikuntlas

Pichikuntlas recite *Basavalingapuranam* (Kunti Malla Reddy Katha) and *Palanati Veera Charitra* to their patron-community i.e. Reddys, Kammas and Kapus. The *Basavalingapuranam* explains the origin of Pichikuntlas and the origin and evalution of their patron-community.

Basavalingapuranam

Basavalingapuranam takes us back into the times when the Universe was created with the birth of Ekonarayana. Then the whole Universe was water. There was neither the earth, nor the sun, nor other luminaries. Later, *Adishakti* was born and asked Ekonarayana to marry her, but he refused. Then *Adishakti* converted herself into a hen with her *Maya* and touched the foot of Ekonarayana and laid three eggs from which sprang Brahma, Vishnu, Siva and other luminaries like sun, moon and stars. To create mankind these three gods constructed a firepit *(Homagundam)* and chanted *OM,* the primordial sound. This *'yagna'* performed by the Trinity, a Brahmin a Kshatriya, a Vaisya and one Adireddy were born to Brahma, the Creator. Brahma ordered them to go to *Bhuloka* and pursue agriculture for the benefit of humanity. All except Adireddy refused to obey the order of Brahma. Brahma was happy because His youngest son had accepted to do what he was expected. Brahma gave him necessary tools useful in the agricultural operations. This Adireddy became the founder of Kapu community who are engaged in agriculture and other allied fields.

After some years, Adireddy was blessed with two sons. They were Buchi Reddy and Bhujanga Reddy. Buchi Reddy was married to a girl by name Mahalaxmi and Bhujanga Reddy to Taraka Devi. One day Bhujanga Reddy went out for hunting and killed a deer. Lord Siva took objection to the action of Bhujanga Reddy who had indulged himself in hunting ignoring his profession i.e. agriculture. Lord Siva cursed Bhujanga Reddy that he would not have any progeny. Mahalaxmi and Taraka Devi were worried that they could not beget children though many years were elapsed. After much pursuation, Bhujanga Reddy reveals that it was due to the caurse of Lord Siva for his cruel act of hunting a deer. Then, these two ladies worshipped Lord Siva for a long time to forgive them. Lord Siva, pleased by their devotion, blessed them to have progeny. Then Uttama Reddy was born to Mahalaxmi and Malla Reddy to Taraka Devi. Malla Reddy had a congenital deformity. He was lame. So he was known as Kunti Malla Reddy. While Uttama Reddy could grow up well receiving proper education and training, Kunti Malla Reddy lagged behind in education. Due to Physical deformity and lack of education, he could not get a bride from respectable Kapu families. So he was married to a girl from Golla community. Kunti Malla Reddy got five sons. Since he could not pursue agriculture or any other allied occupation due to his physical disability, he prayed to Lord Siva to provide livelihood to him and his family. Then Siva gave him a *Ghanta* (a bell), a *Shanku* (conch-shell), a *Yeddu* (bull) and a *Gajasulam* (an iron spike) and enjoined him to lead a mendicant's life of going about places with the bull and depend on the other Kapus for their livelihood. His progeny are known as the Pichikutlas[3]. Thus, the story explains the origin and evolution of Reddy community and Pichikuntla sub-caste.

Runzas

Runzas recite *Vishwakarmapuranam* or *Mulasthambam* and *Parvathikalyanam* for Vishwabrahmin community. Of all the stories recited by Runzas, the *Vishwakarmapuranam* is most important, because the five professions of Vishwabrahmins and their duties are described in it. Therefore, the Vishwabrahmins are more interested in the *Vishwakarmapuranam*. We find this story not only from the oral transmission from the Runzas but also from books because most of the Vishwabrahmins are educated.

Viswakarmapuranam starts with the creation of Universe. Vishwakarma was born to shape this Universe. He was also called *Panchamukha brahma* (Brahma with five faces) or *Adipurusha*. He created the entire world along with three primeval gods Brahma, Vishnu and Siva. Later *Manu, Maya, Thwashtna, Shilpi* and *Vishwagna* Brahmas sprang from the five faces of Vishwakarma. To *Manu* - the ironsmiths, or the kammaras, to *Maya* - the vadrangis or carpenters, to *Thwashtna*- the bronziers or kancharas, to *Shilpi* - the stonecutters and to *Vishwagna* - the *Ausula* or goldsmiths were born. Vishwakarma explained the rules and regulations related to these five professions. As the progeny of Vishwakarma, these five professions call themselves Vishwabrahmins[4]. Thus, the origin of Vishwabrahmins is described in *Vishwakarmapuranam*. This story is also called *Mulasthambam*. The Runzas explain that Vishwakarma told them this story directly. The Runzas claim that this story is itself a *Mahapurana* which means that this *Purana* was not taken from any other *Puranas*. Based on this story the Runzas claim that the founder of the five communities, Vishwakarma, was infact the Creator of this Universe and so he holds highest position among the other gods and goddesses. This would further explain the significance of these five occupations of *Pancha brahmanas*. In the modern times, many scholars have recorded the oral transmission of this *Mahapurana* and published books with their commentaries[5].

2. Parvathikalyanam

The Runzas also recite *Parvathikalyanam* to Vishwabrahmins. Almost all the Runza artists can perfectly recite *Parvathikalyanam*. This story explains the origin of Runza sub-caste.

According to this story Vishwakarma is requested to provide the drums for the marriage of Parvathi and Parameshwara. Then Vishwakarma killed the giant called Rounjaka and made a Runza, a musical instrument out of the giant's skin which could produce 32 kinds of notes. Those who played this instrument at the time of the auspicious marriage of Siva and Parvathi came to be known as Runzas[6]. Both *Vishwakarmapuranam* and *Parvathikalyanam* refer to the origin of Vishwabrahmin and their dependant sub-caste Runzas.

Kunapulivaru

Kunapulivaru recite *Bhavana Rishi Mahatyam* for Padmasali community. It is also called *Padmapuranam* or *Padmasamhitha*[7]. It explains the origin and evolution of Padmasali community as taken from *Markandeyapuranam*[8]. Along with the origin of Padmsalis, the origin of Kunapuli nomadic tribe is also explained in the *Bhavana Rishi Mahatyam*. They treat it as a sacred *Purana*.

Bhavana Rishi Mahatyam

According to the *Bhavana Rishi Mahatyam*, sage Bhrigu was born to Brahma. Aftersome years Mrukanda was born to Bhrigu. For a long time he was not blessed with a child. Mrukanda prayed to Lord Siva and got a child, who was named Markandeya. But the child had to die at the age of sixteen. Yamadharma Raja came to take the life of Markandeya when he became sixteen. Then

Mrukanda, the father of Markandeya prayed to Lord Siva to save his son. Lord Siva fought Yama and saved the life of Markandeya. Lord Siva ordered Markandeya to perform a sacrifice. From this sacrificial fire sprung Bhavana Rishi, the celestial weaver. With the thread obtained from lotus (*Padma*) situated at Vishnu's navel he made clothes for gods. He married Bhadravati, the daughter of the Sun, who bore him 101 sons. After some years, giant Kaluva who belonged to Vishalaksha city had stolen loom of Bhavana Rishi and made clothes with *nara* (Jute) to all the giants. By knowing this Bhavana Rishi waged a war against giant Kaluva, but he could not succeed. Giant Kaluva sprung to life back many times out of the drops of his blood that fell down while fighting Bhavana Rishi. Then Bhavana Rishi brought an army, by name *Pulisainyam* (army of tigers) from Bhadravathi on the advice of Parvathi. Later, Bhavana Rishi killed giant Kaluva with the help of *Pulisainyam* and produced different colours, out of the dead body of giant Kaluva and made clothes of variety of colours. Later, Bhavana Rishi, allowed the *Pulisainyam* to depend on the Padmasali caste for livelihood[9]. Thus, Kunapulivaru a nomadic tribe has come to stay.

We find *Markandeya Purana* in Sri Venkateshwara Oriental Manuscript Library[10], Tirupathi (record number 994). Narasimha kavi was its author. He belonged to 1580 A.D. He composed it in *Dwipada Manjeera* metre. He explained in the preface that he had written this *Purana* on the request of Padmasalis. He also explained that God Gopala swamy asked him in the dream to dedicate this work to Him.

We also find this story in the collections of Meckanzie. According to Meckanzie's manuscripts, the Bhavana Rishi story was written in 1811 A.D. *Prajothpathi* year, *Asada, Sudda* 2 Saturday. This manuscript claims that it was written by sage Vyasa[11].

Subbanna Shatavadhani wrote a book on *Bhavana Rishi Puranam* in 1969. He mentioned various versions of this *Purana* which are now available in print. According to him the first among the writers of *Bavana Rishi Mahatyam* was one, Puranam Kondaiah, belonging to Kunapuli caste[12]. His work was printed in 1893.

Goudajettis

Goudajettis recite *Goudapuranam* and *Surabhandeshwara Katha* to explain the origin of Gouda community. Goudas pay much attention towards these stories.

1. Goudapuranam

Goudapuranam traces the origin of Gouda caste and their dependant sub-castes Goudajettis and Enutivaru to an ancient sage Koundinya, who was born to Lord Brahma. Sage Koundinya, beget 5 sons and one daughter with the blessings of Brahma. They were Adi Gouda, Amara Gouda, Veda Gouda, Viprama Gouda, Pungama Gouda and Challama Devi. They were called *Pancha Goudas*. Challama Devi was married to Katamaiah. They were all collectively working for their livelihood. Adi Gouda was producing toddy from palm tree. Amara Gouda was producing toddy from date palm tree. The other brothers, sister and her husband were selling toddy at *Manduva* (a place where toddy was sold).

These Goudas were vegetarians, and they were strictly following caste regulations. As long as they were following their *dharma*, there was no need for them to use implements for toddy tapping. It is even said that in those days, they were not climbing the palm trees for toddy tapping. The trees were bowing down before them to facilitate them. But in course of time, because of their negligence in folllowing their regulations, the palm trees stood upright. Then they prayed to Lord Siva who responded to their prayer and said that the palm trees would not behave as they did previously but the Goudas should climb the trees to get toddy. Further Lord Siva gave them necessary implements to tap toddy from the trees. Whenever the Gouda community was in trouble Lord Siva was responding to their prayers fevourably. The Gouda community was also rescued from the evils of a giant called Rakthatishudu. The *Goudapuranam* gives a very lengthy narration of various episodes pertaining to this community which will be recited for about a week.

Pungama Gouda and Katamaiah became well known for their charity which the other Goudas namely Adi Gouda, Amara Gouda,

Veda Gouda, and Viprama Gouda did not approve. They protested against the charities given by Katamaiah and Pungama Gouda. Katamaiah and Pungama Gouda appealed to them to give charities which they refused and left for another place separating themselves from the joint family. They lost all their property and they were ex-communicated from the caste for their bad deeds. Later, they had to repent for their evil deeds and requested Katamaiah to pardon them. Though they were not allowed to enter the family, they were treated as a dependant sub-caste known as Goudajettis[13].

2. Surabhandeshwara Katha

The *Surabhandeshwara katha*[14] gives us a very interesting story which elevates the Gouda community for their integrity and honesty. There was a Gouda living in Kasi with his wife Dandalika. He was a toddy tapper. His wife Dandalika was known for her beauty. Once she was taking a bath in the river Ganges, when a brahmin chanced to see her. The brahmin was very much attracted to her beauty and he expressed his desire to her. But she said that she was already married to a Gouda and it was not proper for the brahmin to make such a request. But the brahmin could not control his temptation and approached her on the other day with the same proposal. This time he threatend her that he would take his life if she did not oblige to his request. Dandalika was very much worried that if she rejected him, there was a danger of inviting the effects of a horrible sin causing the death of a brahmin scholar, i.e, *Brahma hatya papam* which is the one of the five gravest sins (*Pancha maha patakas*). To avoid such a sin, she invited the brahmin to her house and satisfied his desire. While the brahmin was till in her house, her husband came to the house. For the fear that her husband might kill the brahmin if he was spotted with her, she put the brahmin in a big empty pot of toddy (*Surabhandam*). The Gouda filled the pot with toddy without any knowledge that the brahmin was hiding in it. This caused the death of the brahmin. She told her husband honestly what had happened. She pleaded with her husband to kill her for her sin. Her husband found the brahmin dead in the *Surabhandam*. Gouda realised that he was responsible for the death of the brahmin and so he thought that he is subjected to the evil effects of the *Brahma hatya patakam*. Then Dandalika prayed to Lord Siva to forgive her husband from *Brahma hatya patakam* and also absolve her sin of extra marital relationship. Lord Siva was very much pleased with her purity of thought, word and deed and rose from the same *Surabhandam* in which the brahmin was drowned. Thus, the Gouda couple were blessed by Lord Siva. This story makes the community proud of their character.

Chinduvaru

Jambavapuranam

The *Jambavapurana* as recited by Chindus and Dakkalis the dependant castes of the Madigas explains the various aspects of the pre-creation, creation and evolution of this Universe. This *Purana* has many characteristic features of the *Mahapurana* and it is very close to the *Devibhagavatham* which speaks of the *Adishakti* or the mother of the Trinity - Brahma, Vishnu and Siva. It is said that Brahma and Vishnu had refused to marry her when she proposed and so they were burnt by Her with Her third eye. Later, Lord Siva consented to marry Her on the condition that she should give him Her third eye which could burnt any thing. Having agreed to this, *Adishakti* parted with Her third eye and gave it to Lord Siva. Lord Siva immediately burnt *Adishakti* and gave life to Brahma and Vishnu. *Adishakti* had reborn in three inferior forms of Parvathi, Lakshmi and Saraswathi who were married by Siva, Vishnu and Brahma respectively. With this the creation of Universe has begun. Brahma created all the elements and numerous species in different forms while Jambavantha, who is said to have been created even before the creation of these species, caused the creation of various professions and the tools necessary to carryout these professions. The Madiga community trace their origin to this Jambavantha who is considered the founder of their caste[15]. *Jambavapurana* is recited as enacted from a stage following the theatrical narration. It is very popular among the lowest strata of the society.

Pandavulavaru

Yayathi Charitra

Pandavulavaru as suggested by the very name of this sub-caste narrate the story of *Maha Bharatha* in as much detail as wanted by the patron-community. They, further, trace their origin to the times of *Vanaparvam* of *Maha Bharatha*. The story relating to their origin was already described in Chapter-III. They recite the *Yayathi Charitra* to the benefit of their patron-community Mutrasis. This story of Yayathi is the same as available in the *Itihasa* and the *Mahapurana* except for its narration regarding the origin of four castes i.e. Mutrasis, Gollas, Bestas and Netakani[16]. Yayathi's children through his four wives Devayani, Shermistha, Nilavathi and Padmini have become the founders of these four castes respectively. This story establishes a very close affinity among these four castes.

Pekkarlu

Pekkaras recite two stories to their patron-community Kummaras (potters). One is *Gundaiah Katha* and the other is *Salivahanapuranam*.

(i) Gundaiah Katha

In *Gundaiah Katha* the origin of the potters caste or Kummaras is described. In this *Purana,* the origin of Kummaras is traced back to the times of the marriage of Lord Siva with Parvathi. For performing this Holy marriage, it was felt that the traditional *Ironi* pots (used even to-day at the time of marriage) were required. Therefore Lord Siva gave life to a clay image of one Gunda Brahma or Gundaiah. Brahma blessed Gundaiah with the art and craft of pottery while Lord Vishnu gave his *Chakra* to him to serve as potter's wheel and Lord Siva gave him his *Gajasula* to stir and mix the mud for making pots. Thus, the caste of potters has come into being. The marriage of Lord Siva with goddess Parvathi was performed during which these *Ironi* pots made by Gundaiah were used. In the earlier stage Gundaiah was making pots with mud. They were not baked in the fire. It is said that a crow damaged a pot made of mud which Gundaiah had hurriedly repaired it using his saliva from his mouth instead of water. Therefore, these pots could not be used for cooking of offerings to the gods. So Lord Siva asked him to bake such pots in fire. Thus, the baked pots have come into being. This story gives us the development of pot making from sun baked pots to the fire baked pots.

This potter Gundaiah was married to Satyavathi with the blessings of Lord Siva. He was a great devotee of Lord Siva. He used to pray to Lord Siva every day before he started his daily routine. One day a prostitute poured unclean water from a house top which fell accidentally on Gundaiah, who was walking in the street. He suddenly chanted the name of Lord Siva. The prostitute realised her mistake and invited Gundaiah to come into her house. She bathed him and washed his clothes and also applied perfumes to him. She worshipped him as the devotee of Lord Siva and then sent him home. Gundaiah's wife, Satyavathi did not know what had happened but suspected her husband that he might have visited a prostitute. She kept him away from her and she was not willing to have marital relationship with her husband. Thus, years passed. The couple became old and infirm. They had no children to support them in their old age. One day sage Narada told Lord Siva about this couple who remained celibate throughout their life. Lord Siva came to their house as a traditional *Jangam* and gave them a pot to preserve with them which he said, he would collect after some days. When Lord Siva in the form of *Jangam* came back after few days to claim his pot, the old couple could not trace it as it disappeared from their house. Lord Siva pretended to be very angry and sent them to *Pathala ganga*. The old couple came out of *Pathala ganga* regaining their youth. They recognised that the *Jangam* was none else than Lord Siva Himself. Lord Siva and Parvathi and all other gods joined together to conduct the marriage of the couple who regained the youth. After this marriage Gundaiah was a blessed with a child and thus the Kummara caste has increased in number[17].

(ii) Shalivahana Charitra

The second story of *Shalivahana Charitra* is related to the times of the Satavahana kings and the famous legendary emperor, Vikramarka of Ujjaini (roughly about 1st and 2nd century B.C.). According to the Shalivahana tradition, Kummaras claim their descent from one Shalivahana, a king of Paithan who was said to be the son of a brahmin father and a Kumbhar mother. According to this story a learned brahmin who wanted to have a good progeny by meeting his wife at an auspicious moment, could not reach his village in time and he was forced to stay with a potter's family for the night. The brahmin requested the potter to give his daughter in marriage to him so that he could get a good son, who could rule a great empire. Thus Shalivahana was born to this learned brahmin through a wife belonging to potter's caste. This son was well versed with art and craft of pottery. He was also blessed with powers of making mounted warriors of earthen figures with whom he could defeat emperor Vikramarka when he invaded South India. Salivahana brought his earthen figures of mounted warriors to life and became the king of that country after expelling king Vikramarka. This Shalivahana is considered to be the founder of ancient royal lines which ruled the Daccan in general and Mysore in particular[18].

The first story of Gundaiah speaks of the origin of the Kummaras who are known as *Desi* Kummaras in the later times and the Shalivahana story created a new branch of Kummaras known as Golkonda Kummaras. The *Desi* Kummaras follow Saivism while Golkonda Kummaras are mostly Vaishnavites. But both these sects would patronise their dependant caste Pekkaras. Their narration unlike the other dependant caste, would throw light not only on the origin of their patron caste but also trace the origin of one of the famous ancient royal lines i.e. the Satavahanas who ruled from Paithan. Unlike the other folklore, this narration make a reference to the legendary emperor Vikramarka whose historicity is not yet established on any firm grounds.

(B) Historical Events

Patamuvaru

Patamuvaru depend on the washers' community or the Rajakas. They recite *Rajakapuranam* or *Basavavijayamu* which describes their origin.

Rajaka Puranam

Rajaka Puranam traces the origin of Rajaka community to the times of destruction of *Daksha Yagna* by Virabhadra. Lord Siva though pleased with the work of Virabhadra ordered him to wash the clothes of gods to absolve the sin of destroying the *Yagna*. Virabhadra created one Madivalu Machaiah to perform the job of washing clothes that explains the founding of the Rajaka community in the ancient times. But the *Purana* brings us to the Medieval times of Bijjala Raju (Chalukyas), who was a Jain. As the story runs, king Bijjala became furious when Madivelu Machaiah and his entire community refused to wash the clothes of Bijjala Raju. Then, the king had sent 84 lakhs pairs of clothes along with an army of 84 lakhs under the command of his brother to the place on the banks of Tripurantakam river where Madivelu Machaiah was living. Madivelu Machaiah not only refused to oblige to request but also cursed the entire army along with the clothes to be burnt by sprinkling the holy ash at them. Thus, the power of the devotee of Siva was proved and the king was taught a lesson. Therefore, this story is also called *Basavavijayamu*.

Basavavijayamu further continues the story to the times of king Prataparudra of Orugallu (1295-1323). Palkurki Somana, a contemporary poet was known for his great work *Basavapuranam*. King Prataparudra who was not a Saivite till then, invited Somana to visit Orugallu and participate in the debate with non-Saivite Brahmins. Palkurki Somana had sent Madivelu Machaiah to debate with the Brahmins instead of participating in it by himself. It is told that the non-Saivite Brahmins were defeated in the religious debate with Machaiah who proved himself a great devotee of Lord Siva. King Prataparudra was convinced about the greatness of the Saivite religion and invited Palkurki Somana to his capital, where the poet was felicitated[19]. This *Basavavijayamu* as recited till to-day by the sub-caste Patamuvaru is available in Sri Venkateshwara Oriental Manuscript Library[20], Tirupathi. Thus, *Rajaka Puranam* being the first part of the narration speaks of the origin of the community while the *Basavavijayamu,* the later part of narration, establishes the supramacy of the Saivite religion and devotion to

Lord Siva. The episode relating to *Basavavijayamu* belong to historical times of early medieval period when Vira Saivism was founded by a great religious reformer, Basava, a contemporary to the king Bijjala of Kalyani (1156 to 1163 A.D.).

Viramustis

The Viramustis a dependant sub-caste of Vaisya community or Komatis sing the story of Kanyaka who is later deified as Vasavi Kanyaka Parameshwari by their community. This story of Vasavi Kanyaka Parameshwari is also known as ***Vaisya Puranam***.

Vasavi Kanyaka Parameshwari Katha

According to the narration of Viramustis, there was a merchant named Kusuma Shetti in a town Penukonda which is situated in the present West Godavari district of Andhra Pradesh. He had a daughter named Kanyaka who was known for her beauty in that region. King Vishnu vardhana, a ruling chief from the city of Rajahmundry, chanced to see her once. Having been attracted by her extraordinary beauty, the king proposed that he was interested to marry her. The parents did not agree to the proposal because it amounted to an intercaste marriage. The entire community disapproved this proposal. The king wanted to marry her even by using force and marched towards Penukonda without a warning. Komatis of Penukonda requested Viramustis who were known for their acrobatic feats to somehow slowdown the pace of king's march so that they could make preparations for a mass immolation. The Viramustis rushed to the king's party and entertained them on the way to Penukonda so that this march was slowed down and the Komatis had time to prepare fire pits for immolation. Watching the disaster, girl Kanyaka cursed the king that his head would be broken into thousand pieces as soon as he entered Penukonda. She had further cursed her own community that the girls born in their community should not be so extraordinarily beautiful as she was so as to avoid such a grave situation in their families. Acknowledging the services of Viramustis who helped their community by slowing down the pace of the kings' army, Kanyaka granted them a boon that they could depend on Vaisya community for their livelihood for generations. After these pronouncements she jumped into fire along with other members of her community and saved themselves from the ignominy of marrying a person who did not belong to thier caste forcibly however great and powerful he might be. Vishnuvardhana reached Penukonda and watched this ghastly scene. Soon his head broke into thousand pieces and died as per the curse of Kanyaka. Since then the Vaisya community started worshipping her as Goddess Vasavi Kanyaka Parameshwari. She has thus become the chief deity of the Vaisya community throughout South India. Viramustis narrate this story to their community along with the description of 101 *Gotras* of Komati families. Penukonda received the attention of this community where Kanyakamma was elevated to the status of a chief goddess of the community. There is a huge temple in that village dedicated to Vasavi Kanyaka Parameshwari and every year celebrations are performed by the community with great zeal and enthusiasm. It has become a pilgrimage centre for this community.

This story, known as *Vaisya Puranam* also, is written in *Dwipada Manjeera* by Guru Bhaskarachary[21] who was encouraged by the community to record the event of the great sacrifice by some of the people of their community to save the honour their community. Kandukuri Veereshalingam had also mentioned this story in his *Kavula Charitra*[22].

As narrated in the story the event centers around a beautiful girl Kanyaka belonging to the merchant community. A king by name Vishnuvardhana wanted to marry her against the wish of Vaisya community. The story cannot be firmly place in a fixed time frame because there were atleast five Vishnuvardhanas[23] among the Chalukyas of Vengi ruling from Rajahmundry including the founder member of line Kubja Vishnuvardhana (624 A.D. to 641 A.D).

These Chalukya kings ruled Rajahmundry from 624 to 1075 A.D. Later Chola-Chalukyas ruled this region from 1076 to about 1200 A.D. These rulers also continued the same pedigree of earlier Chalukya kings which included Vishnuvardhana as one of the titles. Thus, name Vishnuvardhana appears to be the most favoured one in the early Chalukya line which was also continued by the

Chola-Chalukya[24] rulers as a title name. Therefore, it is difficult to identify Vishnuvardhana of *Kanyakaparameshwari katha* with any one of these rulers in the absence of other co-ordinates. Many Andhra historians have opined[25] that Vishnuvardhana (1145 A.D) who donated 25 cows to Virabhadreshwara swamy according to an inscription preserved at a museum in Rajamahendravaram might probably be identified as Vishnuvardhana of the story. The incident might have taken place in about 12th century A.D. This could further be established on the grounds that *Dwipada Manjeera* as a poetic form has been well established by this time and most of the literature of such class is found in this meter and recorded at about the same time.

Pichikuntlas

Pichikuntlas who depend on Reddy, Kamma and Kapu castes recite the story of Battle of Palnadu as *Palnati Vira Bhagavatham* or *Chennudi katha*[26]. This story about a great battle fought at Karempudi in which the families of two half brothers were involved on opposite sides as principals is equated in its greatness with that of the Battle of *Kurukshetra* of the great epic, the *Mahabharatha*.

Palnati Veera Charitra :

Palnati Veera Charitra is much older than the rest of the *Veera ghadhas* (heroic ballads) which are popular in Andhra desha. Some of the European scholars opined that there were no *Veera ghadhas* before 12th century[27] A.D.

The story of *Palnati Veera Charitra* is available in its full form with the troupes of Pichikuntlas. But different troupes of this community recite different parts or episodes of this story. One episode commonly recited by them is *Bala Chandruni Yudda Ghattamu*. Other popular episodes in *Palnati Veera Charitra* are given below[28]. These stories also find a significant place in classical Telugu literature by the noted Telugu poets of the medieval times[29]

According to the story, a king known as Anugu Raju who belonged to Palamachapuri (Jambanapuri, present Jabalpur of Madhya Pradesh) was on his pilgrimage to South India visiting the religious centers in those days. He claimed descent from Karthaviryarjuna, a legendary king of Haihaya dynasty of the pre-Ramayana times. Anugu Raju was advised by a brahmin to wear black colour robes and go for holy dips in the rivers (*Tirthas*) to absolve the sin of their ancestor Karthaviryarjuna who killed sage Jamadagni, father of sage Parashurama. While Anugu Raju visiting the pilgrimage centers for holy dips in the *Tirthas*, his black robes turned white when he had a dip in the Bay of Bengal at Motupalli which indicated that the sin attached to their family was absolved. Therefore, Anugu Raju settled in these parts. During that period the king of Chandavolu, impressed by his valour gave his daughter Mailamadevi in marriage to Anugu Raju besides giving him *Palanati Seema* as dowry. Anugu Raju ruled this region with Gurajala as his capital. He had three wives namely, Viravidyaladevi, Bhuramadevi and Mailamadevi. He got eight sons through these wives. Nalagamudu was the eldest son born to Mailamadevi while Pedda Malidevudu younger to Nalagamudu was born to the eldest wife, the crown queen, Viravidyaladevi.

Doddanaidu was the minister in the service of Anugu Raju. Brahmanaidu was his son. Brahmanaidu succeeded his father and took reins of administration as Prime Minister. After the death of Anugu Raju, Brahmanaidu coronated Nalagama Raju and strove for the unity of the kingdom as desired by Anugu Raju. He prevented the division of the kingdom.

Nagamma, a devotee of Lord Siva belonging to Jittagamalapadu village, had an opportunity to host a grand feast to Anugu Raju who came to those parts for hunting. Being pleased at this treat, Anugu Raju offered to fulfil her desire if any. She requested the king to give her an opportunity to rule his kingdom as Prime Minister for seven *Ghadias* (approximately seven hours). Anugu Raju granted this desire of her and permitted her to claim this whenever she wanted. She reserved this for a future occasion. But she used to frequent to Gurajala and gained influence in the royal court as she had already won the admiration of the king. But Brahmanaidu did not attach any importance to this and paid no special attention to her. Therefore, Nagamma developed a grudge against Brahmanaidu and waited for an occasion to dislodge Brahmanaidu from his premier position. Gradually she developed a firm grip over Nalagama Raju and forced him to divide the kingdom acceding a portion of it to his half brother, Malideva Raju which Brahmanaidu wanted to prevent at any cost. After the division Brahmanaidu had gone to the side of Malideva Raju and served him as Prime Minister at Macherla. Nagamma became Prime Minister of Nalagama Raju at Gurajala. Brahmanaidu strengthened the kingdom of Macherla by inviting a matrimonial alliance from king Veera Somana of Kalyani Chalukya line (1165-1177 A.D).

Later, with the evil intension of dislodging Brahmanaidu even from Macherla and to unite the kingdom under Nalagama Raju by expelling Malideva Raju from Macherla by foul means Nagamma invited Brahmanaidu to participate in a cock-fight contest. Brahmanaidu lost the game due to the treachery of Nagamma. He and Malidevaraju were made to live in forest for seven years. After the expiry of this period as per the agreement Brahmanaidu sent his envoy to claim Macherla from Nalagamaraju which was rejected. Then preparations were started for the great battle. In the Battle of Karempudi the son of Brahmanaidu, by name Balachandrudu, fought valiantly and lost his life. Brahmanaidu won the battle and Nagamma fled from the field. Later, Brahmanaidu seated Nalagama Raju the lone survivor of the familyon the throne and withdrew to forests renunciating the world.

Thus, the story of *Palnati Veera Charitra* depicts the honesty, dedication and righteous conduct of Brahmanaidu and the heroic fight of Balachandrudu against the cunning politics of Nagamma. It explains how the kingdom disintegrated due to the selfish and degenerated politics. The story of Balachandrudu for his heroic fight has been projected prominently by the scholars in their works.

The historicity of Anugu Raju who hailed from North India claiming descent from ancient Haihaya dynasty and their settlement in Andhra and the great war were discussed by a number of scholars in their research works. Though it is believed that he had come and settled down in Andhra, the names of his wives and sons and the then ministers resemble the native names. Perhaps the ancestors of Anugu Raju, a number of generations before his rule, might have come and settled in this region.

Haihayas, in the beginning ruled the region between Jabalpur and Nagapur in the north of Andhra region[30]. Gradually they migrated to Andhra region and ruled over *Konaseema* and *Palnadu* areas. The inscriptions issued by their dynasty are found between 1128 and 1209 in *Konaseema* region. We do not have sufficient evidence to know when the rule of Haihayas was started in the *Palnati seema*. Some inscriptions which belonged to 12th century A.D. indicate their rule in this region[31].

Haihayas were the subordinates of Western Chalukyas. They helped Tribhuvana Malla Vikramaditya (1076-1126 A.D.), the Western Chalukyan king in his Vengi expedition which took place in 1118 A.D. Thus it is believed that Haihayas were ruling over Palnadu region during that period.

Based on the inscriptions found in this region the geaneology of Haihaya dynasty is attempted by Pingali Laxmikantham in his book as given in appendix-v.

The story of *Palnati Veera Charitra* contains three important historical references.

(a) The acquisition of Palnadu, by Anugu Raju after marrying the daughter of Chandavolu Raja.

(b) The marriage of Malideva Raju with daughter of Kalyani Someshwara.

(c) The rulers who participated or sent military assistance to one of the parties in the Battle of Karempudi.

Because of the first event as mentioned above the rivalry between Palnati Haihayas and Velanati Cholas came to an end. The second event indicated the matrimonial relation between Kalyani Chalukya kings and Haihayas. Because of this, the Velanati Cholas, on behalf of the Nalagama fought against Malideva who was supported by Kalyani kings. Rudradeva (or Prataparudra) had sent about one thousand cavalry to take part in the Battle of Karempudi.

According to *Kallu Pratishtha* episode, Nalagama Raju invited his contemporary rulers Bheema of Dharanikota, Ketha Raju of Kota and Prataparudra-I (or Rudradeva) of Kakatiya dynasty (1157-1195 A.D.)[32].

Bheemaraju-II of Dharanikota ruled between 1153-1182 A.D. Kota Ketha Raju of Dharanikota was son of Bheema Deva-II, who went to Brahmana on behalf of Nalagama Raju as mediater to avoid the war. Kakati Prataparudra-I or Rudradeva (1157-1195 A.D.) who started his reign in 1157 A.D. defeated Bheema of Dharanikota in 1182 and made his son Kotaraju-II as his subordinate ruler. Three personalities lived during the period 1153 and 1182. Therefore, the Battle of Palnadu with all probability, might have taken place around 1182 A.D[33].

Mandahechus

The Mandahechus tell the story of Katamaraju who was the last of the Yadava lineage of chiefs. The story of Katamaraju is also known as *Yadavabharathamu*, *Gollabharathamu* and *Yadusastramu*[34]. The long story of Katamaraju is very popular among the lower strata of the society at places like Darsi, Kanigiri, Kandukuru, Udayagiri of Nellore and Prakasham districts. They are also popular in Guntur, Cuddapah and Kurnool districts. However, the Golla community all over the state take pride in Katamaraju as their hero.

Katamaraju Katha

Katamaraju story is in the form of a long verse transmitted orally from generation to generation. The story speaks about three generations of Yadava chiefs culminating in the Battle of Erragaddapadu. The narration contains about 21 stories with historical facts pertaining to the Yadava chiefs belonging to

Yelamanchili region of present Vishakapatnam district, who later migrated to the region of Nellore and Prakasham districts in the south.

The foregoing account of the history of the Yadava chiefs is collected from the narration of the Mandahechu families visitig the Telangana districts of Andhra Pradesh.

The Mandahechus sing the ballads of Katamaraju to the Golla community for a number of days camping in a village. After offering the traditional prayers to Ganapathi, Donakonda Ganga and Mallanna they begin the narration with the life of Avula Valuraju who was the Yadava chief of Yelamanchili in Vishkhapatnam district. His parents were Kariyavula Ganguraju and Gangamma. He had three brothers, namely Harigopala, Nandagopala and Govardhana.

Avula Valuraju picked up a quarrel with one of his neighbouring chiefs, Kalabuta Ganguraju of Kandemondemula kota by promising protection to the latter's ministers who were to be punished by their chief on charges of corruption. All his brothers died fighting the chief of Kandemondemula kota. Avula Valuraju had 5 sons and one daughter. He also left for the battle field after arranging the succession of his second son, Peddiraju to the estate. Valuraju also died in the battle.

Peddiraju ruled Yelamanchili for about 10 years and then moved to Pampadri with his brothers where he ruled for seven years. Since he had no children he divided his property of cows, gold, jewellary and other valuables among his brothers and left for Kalyana Pattanam (modern Karnataka) where he got a son, Katamaraju and a daughter, Papanuka. He died in a battle fighting his enemy, Valiketuvaraju, who was later killed by Katamaraju. As a strange co-incidence all the brothers of Peddiraju also died fighting their enemies in separate engagements. Later, Baktiranna, son of Poluraju, the youngest of the brothers, took initiative to bring the third generation back to Yelamanchili. Thus, Katamaraju and Papanuka also came back to Yelamanchili. Katamaraju ascended the throne of Yelamanchili.

After some time Katamaraju moved with his cattle to Srisailam and turned towards Nellore where Nallasiddi was ruling at the time. Katamaraju was warned by his kinsmen not to go towards Nellore because Mukkanti of Nellore had killed his uncle Poluraju. Despite the warning, Katamaraju entered into an agreement with Nallasiddi on the payment of grazing tax which led to a fresh trouble between Katamaraju and Nallasiddi. In a battle that followed Katamaraju killed Nallasiddi and avenged the death of his uncle but he had also succumbed to his injuries in the war.

Thus, the narration culminates in the death of Katamaraju who occupied a place of pride in the minds of Yadavas. The story assumed the status of a *Purana* and an epic. Katamaraju is praised by the Yadavas as the incarnation of Lord Krishna.

Though the legend of Katamaraju traces his family pedigree from Lord Krishna, various traditional literary sources differ with one another regarding the number of generation to which he belonged beginning from Lord Krishna. According to various sources, the number of generations between Lord Krishna and Katamaraju ranges between 11 and 23[35]. However, the last three generations consisting Valuraju, Peddiraju and Katamaraju are not disputed by any source. The historicity of these three chiefs in succession can be corroborated with the epigraphic and other literary sources.

The date of the engagement which took place between Katamaraju and Nallasiddi at Erragaddapadu is very crucial in fixing the chronology of these three generations preceding Katamaraju.

Various scholars suggested different dates for the decisive Battle of Erragaddapadu. The first among the scholars who applied historical method to arrive at the date of the battle is Varanasi Yashoda Devi[36]. She suggested in her thesis submitted to Madras University that the battle took place in 1259 A.D. between Nallasiddi and Katama Raju at Erragaddpadu near Panchalingala konda. She claimed that Manmasiddi-III (1248-67) was also known as Nallasiddi who waged war against Katamaraju on the question of grazing tax (*pullari*). She based her argument on an inscription found at

Gundlapalem village in Kandukuru Taluq of Prakasham district. Her opinion was countered by the later researchers who doubted the authenticity of the said inscription because the Saka year *Kalayukthi* and the names of the month, the date, the *thithi* were proved to be wrong after verification. Secondly, the oral narrative of Mandahechus mention clearly that the year of the engagement was *Chitrabhanu* (Telugu year).

Timmawajjala Kodanda Ramaiah[37], a Telugu scholar wrote an article on Katamaraju which was published in Bharathi in 1953. He mentioned that C.P. Brown noticed the story of Katamaraju while he was persuing Mackenzie's manuscripts in Mackenzie library. The Mackenzie collections mention that the year of the battle was 1081 of Salivahana Saka corresponding to 1157 A.D. The year 1157 A.D. is neither *Kalayukthi* as mentioned in the inscription or *Chitrabhanu* as told by the narrators. Secondly, the Mackenzie collections were mostly based on hearsay with regard to the events of the distant past. Though the year may not be taken for granted, the event might be ascribed to the period around 1157 A.D.

Mallampally Somasekhara Sharma, a wellknown research scholar in Andhra history, wrote an introduction to Katamaraju katha edited by Veturi Prabhakara Sastri who brought to light the palm-leaf manuscripts of this story preserved in the Oriental Manuscript Library, Madras[38]. He questioned the authenticity of Gundlapalam inscription on the grounds that the saka year mentioned in the inscription was not corresponding to the Telugu month and year as stated in the inscription itself. He traced the year of the battle to 1163 A.D. wich satisfies the Telugu year, month, day and the *thithi* as narrated by Mandahechus and also as mentioned in the palm-leaf manuscript preserved in Oriental Manuscript Library, Madras. But he could not conclude this fact as he entertained a doubt that Khadga Tikkana who was mentioned as a great hero of this Battle on the side of Nallasiddi, belonged to a much later date at least about a hundred years hence.

Another scholar, Devurapalli Venkata Krishna Reddy suggested that the engagement between Katamaraju and Nallasiddi took place on 17-03-1282[39] A.D. (S.S.[40] 1204 *Chitrabhanu Kartika bahula* 14 Saturday) on the strength of an inscription found at Narsaraopet (1203 S.S. *Vishnu, Kartika sudda* 2 Thursday correspondig to 16-10-1281 A.D.). This inscription gives chronology of the Telugu Choda rulers who ruled from Nellore. Nallasiddi who was mentioned in a genealogy of Choda rulers in this inscription was identified by the scholar as the one who fought Katamaraju on *pullari* issue. But the said inscription neither mentions the agreement on *pullari*, nor any reference regarding the actual reign of the said Nallasiddi. Further, the date given by him as 17-03-1282 does not correspond to the other details of ***Chitrabhanu*** year such as month, date and day. He identifies Nallasiddi to be the same as narrated in the palm-leaf manuscript on the ground that the writer of inscription was one, Tikkana, who was a writer, poet, minister and also commender-in-chief to Nallasiddi. But Nallasiddi's predecessor Manmasiddi was ruling upto 1290 A.D. Therefore 1282 cannot be taken as the date for the engagement in which both Nallasiddi and Katamaraju died fighting each other.

In his Doctoral thesis submitted to Osmania University, Hyderabad, K. Mohan Rao suggested that the war between Nallasiddi and Katamaraju was fought for eight days starting from 23-11-1282 and the final engagement took place on 1-12-1282 A.D[41]. As the Telugu day does not correspond to the Telugu month *Magha* of *Chitrabhanu* year as recited by the Mandahechus the scholar opines that the narrators are mistaking *Margasira* month for the *Magha* month of the *Chitrabanu*[42]. If it was *Margasira* month the day (Tuesday) and the *thithi* (Amavasya) fall on 01-12-1282 A.D. This suggestion is also based on his mere imagination because in the formal oral narration, the narrators seldom commit any corruption as it happens generally in the written records while they are copied. Secondly, the traditional ceremonies in memory of the fallen heroes are celebrated during the months of *Magha - Vaishaka*. Annual fairs at Ganga Donakonda, Prakasham district are conducted during the month of Chaitra[43] every year. The last rites of the dead Yadava rulers were performed by one Baktiranna, who was the only survivor of the battle as he was away in Kasi during the war.

Perhaps it might have taken one or two months for him to return to this place from Kasi and found that his kith and kin were killed in the battle. On knowing this, he might have performed the ritual in the month of *Chaitra* for about six days commencing from full moonday. These days even now are celebrated every year as important fairs dedicated to their goddess Ganga. Therefore, the battle might have taken place in and around the month of *Magha*. Therefore the *Margasira* could not be mistaken as *Magha*.

Now let us examine the source material available on the conflict between Yadava chiefs and their contemporary rulers of the plains. These sources may be classified as :

(a) Palm-leaf manuscripts

(b) Kaifiyats

(c) Inscriptions

(d) Customs and rituals

(e) Oral narrations

(a) Palm - leaf manuscripts

The palm-leaf manuscripts scattered in Andhra area and possesed by a number of leading narrators of the Yadava folklore, were callected by Mackenzie and preserved in the Madras Oriental Manuscript Library. These manuscripts were brought to light by Charles Philips Brown with his comments and remarks at relevant places. These notes along with the manuscripts were re-examined and edited by Veturi Prabhakara Sastri. The Oriental Manuscripts Library, Madras published a volume entitled "Katamaraju katha" with detailed introduction of Mallampalli Somasekhara Sharma (1953). This book contains minor episodes of *Battu rayabharamu Kotapati thati vrikshamu Techekatha*, *Erragaddapati potlata* besides the story of Katamaraju. Later, T.Subba Rao has collected some more manuscripts from the Yadava story tellers and published them in 1976.

Still a number of old copies of palm-leaf manuscripts are available with the story tellers. Number of writers copied them in course of time. We come across seven versions of such manuscripts[44]. The most important fact about the Yadava story tellers is that they were and are illiterates. Each head of the family had to make copies of the manuscripts he possessed and distributed them to all his sons who also shared the inherited *Mirasi* villages. Their sons divide themselves into separate independant units of story telling groups after acquiring a copy of the manuscript and a set of musical instruments. Surprisingly their oral narrations are not necessarily based on the manuscript they possess.

All the copies of palm-leaf manuscript unanimously decree that the final battle of Katamaraju with Nallasiddi was held on *Magha Amavasya* Tuesday of *Chitrabhanu* year.

This final engagement was preceded by a war between the Yadavas and Nallasiddi forces commencing from *Magha Bahula Dashimi*. Thus the war continued for six days culminating in the death of Katamaraju and Nallasiddi on the day of *Amavasya*, Tuesday. The manuscripts further mention that one Baktiranna, the lone survivor of the family, who was away in Kasi returned home and found that all his kinsmen were killed in the battle. Then he performed the last rites to the departed. The manuscripts do not tell us the difinite year in the Saka era The mention of the names of the cyclic year *Chitrabhanu* which is repeated every sixty years, poses great difficulty in identifying the exact date of the engagement. The day, *thithi*, month and year of *Chitrabhanu* would only match with the date 05-02-1163[45] of the Christian era.

The stylistics of the written folklore in *Dwipada Manjeera* may give us a clue about the period when it was composed. The *Dwipada* metre is used in Telugu literature at least from 8th and 9th centuries as found in the Telugu inscriptions of that period. The Dwipada metre seems to be widely prevalent in composition of the Telugu folklore between 9th and 14th centuries. The type of literature was prepared by the folklorists because of its adoptability for singing. This type of literature must have reached its height of popularity in the 12th century when Katamaraju story and the Battle of Palanadu were composed in *Dwipada Manjeera* and sung by the begging communities througout the Andhra region. This would suggest that the Battle of Erragaddapadu might have occurred in mid 12th century. Though the two battles were held in the same century, we do not find any reference of the other engagement in either of the stories. It may be due to the fact that the causes of these two Battles were different. While the Battle of the Erragaddapadu was fought on the question of *pullari*, the other Battle of Palanadu was fought on account of the jealousy between two half brothers who ruled the divided kingdom. Secondly, the Battle of Erragaddapadu was fought between the pastoral chiefs, the Yadavas and the rulers of the civilized plains. Therefore, the Katamaraju story was popular among the Yadavas who constituted the lowest strata of society whereas the Battle of Palanadu was more popular among the other community. The similarity of these stories may be found in using the same meter for composing the songs to glorify and narrate these two heroic events of the Telugu speaking people.

(b) Kaifiyats

Mackenzie's kaifiyats pertaining to Pattapuravi, Siddavatam, Kumbhagiri etc. mention the Battle of Erragaddapadu. These kaifiyats give descriptions of the battle between Nallasiddi and Katamaraju on the question of the non-payment of *Pullari* by Katamaraju and causing damage to the cattle of Katamaraju by Nallasiddi during the period of severe famine. Besides the cause of the *Pullari*, these kaifiyats also mention the petty cause as an immediate one preceding the deadly Battle. A pet parrot of Kundamadevi, wife of Nallasiddi, was shot with an arrow by Poluraju, an uncle of Katamaraju. The Boyas who had a grouse with the Yadavas because they were deprived of their livelihood as Yadavas cleared the jungles off wild animals, took an advantage of this. The Boyas under the instruction of the queen, killed some of the cattle of the Yadavas. Since the Yadavas lost theirs precious cattle, they refused to pay *pullari* to Nallasiddi. This had led to the battle of Erragaddapadu according to these kaifiyats. These kaifiyats were compiled at least 6 or 7 centuries after the engagement and they depended on hearsay. Though they donot help us in fixing the exact date of the Battle, they give a clear account of the cause and course of the Battle besides the description of various rituals attached to the anniversary of this war.

(c) Inscription

The lone inscriptional source which speaks of the Battle of Erragaddapadu is an undated inscription found at Gundlapalem near Kandukuru of Prakasham district. On four sides of a stone pillar, the account of the Battle was inscribed with very little variance. As this inscription copies the relevant poems from *Andhra Bharatham* and Pothana's *Bhagavatham*, the inscription might have been composed during or after 15th century. Therefore, this inscription might have also been based on the hearsay account.

The inscription made an attempt to glorify the history of Yadavas by linking Katamaraju with that of Yadava chiefs beginning from the epic hero Lord Krishna. It also attempted to fix the date of the battle at 3965 of Kali age which means 863-64 of Christian era which was also a *Chitrabanu* year according to the Telugu calender. But the same inscription also gives a definite date of the Battle as the *Kalayukti, Kartika, Suddha Panchami*, Thursday of 1170 Saka era (1248 A.D.). Correspondingly 1170 of saka era was not *Kalayukti* but it was *Keelaka*. Both of these years are intervened by 8 years. Surprisingly the inscription ignores the *Chitrabhanu* year which is popularly mentioned in the folklore. As the four sides of the inscription are the copies of the same account with a little difference in their introductory and concluding paragraphs, these sides might have been inscribed at different intervals by the admirers of the Yadavas[46].

(d) Customs and Rituals

Gangamma or Ganga Bhavani is worshiped as chief deity by the Yadavas and other sections of the lower strata of the society in Prakasam district in general and Darsi taluka in particular. Many villages have small temples built for Goddess Ganga who is believed to be the protector of the cattle. Donakonda Ganga is still the most popular deity in the region drawing thousands of devotees every year during the fair held from *Chaitra Suddha Dashimi* to *Bahula*

Thadiya which falls generally in the month of March/April. Besides Donakonda, the fairs are also held for the Goddess Ganga at Paleti, Peda Alavalapadu, Darsi, Samanthapadi, Somavarapadu of Prakasham district and Kurnool, Cuddapah districts. These fairs are also held in *Chaitra* or *Vaishakha* months. During these fairs[47] the *Yadava Bharathamu* is recited by begging sub-caste *Kommu Gollas* and *Pikilivaru*. The Mandahechus are not given any jurisdiction over this region to conduct recital though they attend these fairs in large number. Their jurisdiction is limited to Telangana districts only.

As a part of major rituals, the death of Yadava heroes is also celebrated by organising the procession of the *Prabhas* and offering *Bonalu* to the Goddess.

The deity, Donakonda Ganga is the most prominent among others because it is believed that the Yadavas could migrate to the southern regions with her blessings. Secondly the final battle was fought at Erragaddapadu in the proximity of Donakonda. Thirdly, after the battle, the Yadavas returned to Donakonda and supposed to have cleaned their swords or weapons in the Paleru stream running by the side of the Ganga temple.

Fourthly, it is also believed that the Yadavas had buried their weapons at the temple after the war was over. Baktiranna, the lone survivor, performed the last rites to the dead on the banks of the Paleti river. Therefore, Donakonda occupies a very imortant place in the psyche of the Yadavas.

During these fairs the Yadavas also conduct a unique ceremony known as *Avula pabbam* in memory of those cattle which lost their lives in the battle fighting in favour of the Yadavas. This particular ceremony is peculiar to Rayalaseema region only. During this offering to the cattle, the heroic role played by the cattle in the war is described by the story tellers. In particular they speak about the contribution of *Bollavu*. The cattle also receive the honour and recognition on par with the dead Yadava heroes. This would reveal that the cattle were generally used in the warfare in the Offensive strategies.

(e) Oral Narrations

The Mandahechus belong to a nomadic tribe of the Yadavas who would recite the history of the Yadava chiefs, particularly their wars with other rulers of the plains. They visit the villages under their jurisdiction once in two or three years and give their performance only to the Yadava community. They take donations for their livelihood from the Yadavas. They also keep the family particulars of the Yadava house-holds. The Mandahechus would permanently stay in a few villages and visit other villages ascribed to them in compact units. The different groups keep a copy of the manuscript of the Yadava stories irrespective of the fact whether they are literates are not. However, the narrators do not differ with each other. The text of oral narration is a dramatic version of the content presented in the kaifiyats. The narrators would memorise the texts. But, however, they may present some illustrations which may or may not conform with the major story. Such digressions are attempted by the story tellers to keep the audience in good humor as they sit for long hours during the day or night. These narrations also do not speak the exact date of the event or the causes of the struggle in a precise and objective manner. They also suffer from the exaggeration. These apart, they serve as a good historical account of the nature of the problems. The texts of the oral literature would reveal that the story is composed in *Dwipada Manjeera*, the metre and the rhythm of which are suitable for singing. The presentation of the text in meter form would prevent the interpolations and facilitate a truthful rendering.

On verification of the oral accounts of the different troupes of the Mandahechus, it is found that they follow a uniform method, form and content with regard to their performances among their communities. There is no difference of opinion among these troupes in describing that the final battle at Erragaddapadu between Katamaraju and Nallasiddi was held on *Magha, Amavasya* Tuesday of *Chitrabhanu* year. One of the most interesting things to be observed in their presentation of facts is that the narrators give equal priority to both the rival groups in the description of their valour.

All the oral narratives specify clearly the day of the final engagement beween Katamaraju and Nallasiddi[48] as Tuesday *Magha Amavasya* of *Chitrabhanu* which correspondingly falls on 5-2-1163[49].

The kaifiyats and the oral narratives differ with each other in identifying the important cause of the trouble. The kaifiyats mention that Katamaraju's cattle caused damage to the crops. But they gave more importance to a personal reason that the Yadavas killed a pet parrot of queen Kundamadevi[50]. The oral narratives also mention that the Yadavas' cattle caused damage to the crops but they alleged that this was only a retaliation to the damage done to their cattle by the Boyas under the order from Kundamadevi. Inspite of this, the Yadava story tellers do not find fault with either Katamaraju or Nallasiddi by stating that Katamaraju did not know that Kundamadevi was not informed by Nallasiddi of the *Pullari* agreement. Similarly the narrators also absolve Nallasiddi on the ground that Nallasiddi was not aware of the damage caused to the cattle by the Boyas and that they declared war on the Yadavas for damaging crops. Thus, the oral narratives would suggest that the misunderstanding based on misinformation was the real cause of the trouble. Otherwise, both the parties had respect for their agreement.

Before the commencement of war, Nallasiddi sent one person by name Raya Shrungavali (*Battu*) as his representative to Katamaraju demanding the payment of *Pullari* and to serve a warning of direct action if Katamaraju failed to do so. Katamaraju did not agree to pay the tax but challenged Nallasiddi's claim for the same disregarding the damage done to his cattle.Since the conciliatory efforts proved to be futile, both the parties made preparations for the war. Nallasiddi and Katamaraju sent messages to their respective kith and kin besides the friendly chiefs to join their sides.

The actual engagement according to oral narratives began on Thursday, Bahula Dashimi (correspondingly 30-1-1163). The oral narratives and the kaifiyats describe the battle which took place between Khadga Tikkana, a minister of Nallasiddi and Challa Pinnamanidu, brother of Katamaraju on one day and with Brahmarudraiah a minister of Challa Pinnamanidu on the following day resulting in the heroic death of both the Brahmin ministers preceding the commencement of the actual engagement.

The oral narratives give clear description of the war which took about 6 days. On the first day (30-1-1163 A.D.). Komarasiddi, brother of Nallasiddi, led the army against Katamaraju's force led by Katamaraju's brother, Challa Pinnamanidu, in which the commanders of both sides lost their lives. On the second day (1-2-1163 A.D.) the Bollavu, a God-gifted cow, caused heavy damage to Nallasiddi's army and by the close of the day, the cow was killed by the Boyas who joined the side of Nallasiddi.

Birnidu, another brother of Katamaraju, commanded the Yadava force on the third day (2-2-1163 A.D.) and died a heroic death.

Itamaraju, another brother of Katamaraju, fought against Kasthurisiddi and Errasiddi, brothers of Nallasiddi on the fifth day (3-2-1163 A.D.) and all the three of them lost their lives on the battle field.

Avula Yerraiah, another brother of Katamaraju, led Yadava force on the sixth day (4-2-1163 A.D) and met the same fate as his predecessors.

The war had so far deplenished the resources in men and material on both sides. Katamaraju and Nallasiddi both had lost all their brothers and close relatives in the war but still they preferred a final battle which should be decisive - since they had lost most of their men, each one of them was not interested any more in the victory. Since Katamaraju was childless, his brother Itamaraju had already sent his son Alludhadenna, to a distant place, Katakam (Ganjam) with a small force to continue their lineage irrespective of the results of the war. On the final day (5-2-1163 A.D.) Katamaraju killed Nallasiddi in the battle and he also succumbed to the injuries later.

Sum up

The narrations of these nomadic tribes generally have two major components. Firstly, they tried to trace the origin of their patron-caste and the origin of their sub-caste, from the ancient

Puranic lore, now known as *Kulapuranas*. These legends do not however, conform with any of the classical *Puranas* known as *Asthadasa Mahapuranas* composed by Vedavyasa. These *Kulapuranas* are like *Sthalapuranas* written about the antiquity and significance of pilgrimage centers and narrating pre-historic episodes to substantiate their claim. These legendary accounts explain their origins by tracing the founding fathers of their communities who were directly connected to either Lord Siva or Brahma or Mahashakthi of the times immediately after the Universe is created, in some cases to the times prior to the Creation.

The second major component of their narrations constitute one or more than one episodes relating to their communities during the early medieval times. Some of the major battles fought by their ancestors in the early medieval period are also sung by these dependant nomadic tribes so that the present generations of their communities could take pride in their great ancestors. These narrations are very close to the historical events of those times. The contemporaneity of the participatory chiefs in a battle would help us locate these events in more or less a definitive historical frame of time and space. Thus, the oral narrations of these nomadic tribes help us reconstructing the history of that period.

References

1. Subramanyam, G.V. , **Purana Vagmayam**, Hyderabad - p. 55.
2. Levistraus. Claud, Structural Anthropology c.f. P. Subba chari.
3. Sitikela Ramulu, President, A.P. Pichikunti Society, Mahaboobnagar district narrated this story on 06-08-1995.
4. Personal interview with Pasham Somasekhar, a Runza artist, 60 years old, Garla Village, Khammam district on 18-08-1999.
5. Niranjana Sastri's ***Vishwakarma Brahmana Vamshagamanamu*** explains the derivation of these ***Panchabrahmanas*** (five professions). Dr. Konduri Raghavacharyulu had written a book on ***Vishwakarma Puranam*** explaining the five professions, the creation of Universe, the ***Sutras*** and ***Gotras***, the incarnation of

Vishwakarma, 18 ***Yugas***, 18 ***Munis*** and the ethical codes of society. We also find another work on Vishwakarma in Telugu of Veevuri Venkatacharyulu. He also explained the five professions and the creation of the Universe by Vishwakarma.

6. Pasham Somasekhar, a Runza artist, 60 years old, Garla village, Khammam District, on 18-08-1999.
7. Personal interview, with Bikshapathi, 45 years old, a Kunapuli artist, Sayampeta village, Warangal district on 17-08-1999.
8. But ***Markandeyapuranam*** does not make a mention of this story of Kunapulivaru. This story is known as ***Padmasali kula yachaka puranam***.
9. Personal interview with Venkateshwar, a Kunapuli, 50 years old, Vijayawada, on 17-09-1998.
10. Seetha Devi, P., **Dwipada Sahitya Charitra**, Hyderabad, pp. 412 - 416.
11. Subbanna Shatavadhani, C.V, **Bhavana Rishi Puranam**, Podduturu, 1969 p. 9.
12. *Ibid.*
13. Akula Venkataiah, a Goudajetti artist, 60 years old, Mulugu village, Warangal district narrated this story on 19-08-1998.
14. Personal interview with Akula Venkataiah, a Goudajetti artist, Mulugu village, Warangal district on 19-08-1998.
    The story is available in **Dwipada Manjeera** meter written by a poet Guruvaiah, who belonged to 16th or 17th c. A.D. The Manuscripts is preserved in the Madras Oriental Manuscript Library (R.No. 1207). The oral narration of the above respondent tallies with the text of this Manuscript.
15. Chindula Yellaiah, 60 years old, Armoor, Nizamabad district, narrated this story on 17-8-1999.
16. Netakanis are found in a small number in the hilly regions of Adilabad, Karimnagar and Warangal districts. They collect fruits of forest and sell in the towns like Mutrasis. They look like tribals.
17. Personal interview with Paidipala Agaiah, a potter, 72 years old, Hanamkonda, Warangal district on 17-10-1999.
18. Thurston, E. *op. cit.*, p. 113.
19. Induri Kotaiah, a Patamu artist, 63 years old, from Ganapuram village, Warangal district narrated this story on 19-5-1997.
20. The present version of **Basavavijayamu** was written by

Nallanagadda Naranaradhyudu in **Dwipada Manjeera** metre as preserved in Sri Venkateshwara Oriental Manuscript Library Record No. 565.

21. Madras Oriental Manuscript Library Document No. 1011 as quoted from T. Susheela, in **Andhra Dwipada Sahitya Charitra**, Hyderabad, 1977, p. 435.
22. Venkata Krishna Rao. Bhava raju, **Sri Raja Raja Narendra Pattabhi Sekha Sanchika**, Rajamahendravaramu, 1924, p. 143.
23. See appendix-III.
24. See appendix-IV.
25. Raja gopala Rao. Tekumalla , South Indian research, c.f. Venkata Krishna Rao. Bhava raju, *op. cit.*, p. 148.
26. Subba Rao, T., **Katama Raju Kathalu**, Vol. I, Hyderabad, 1976, p. xxv.
27. *Ibid.*
28. Anuguraju Palanati samvadamu,
    Palanati Rajya vibhagamu,
    Kollaporu - Gopana virugu
    Aranya vasamu or Mandadi valasa
    Mandapotu - Lankanna virugu
    Gurajala yuddamu
    Alaraju Rajyabharamu
    Kallu Pratistha
    Bala Chandruni Yuddhamu
    Komma raju Yuddhamu
    Brahmana virugu
    Pingali Laxmikantham, **Palnati Vira Charitra**, Vol. I, Hyderabad, 1976, p. xxv.
39. Srinatha : Kallu Pratishta, Balachandruni Yuddham.
    Mallaiah : Kollaporu, Gopanna Virugu.
    Kondaiah : Kommaraju Yuddhamu.
    Tangirala Venkata Subba Rao has collected 25 stories related to ***Palnati Veera Charitra*** from Guntur district. In the year 1862 a book was authored by Virabhadrakavi of Palnadu, entitled as ***Virabhagavathamu*** in which he narrated ***Palnati katha chakram*** in a comphrehensive manner. The palm-leaf manuscripts preserved in the Madras Oriental Manuscript Library (Document Number 1112 to 1120) and Sri Venkateshwara

Oriental Manuscript Library, Thirupati also give details about the ***Palnati Veera Charitra*** and the events related to it.

30. Pingali Laxmikantham, op.cit., p. xii

31. According to them Beta Raju in the beginning of 12th century, another Betha Raju in 1128 A.D., who were also called Birudankarudra, and Kamaraju (Anugu Raju) in 1147 A.D. ruled this region. Later, Malidevaraju, son of Viravidyaladevi, Nalagama Raju, son of Mailamadevi also ruled this region but the time of their rule was not mentioned in the inscriptions.

32. ధరణి కోట పురికి దక్షుడైనట్టి
భీమదేవుండను పృధ్వీశునకును (కల్లు ప్రతిష్ఠ కథ - **1106 - 1107** పంక్తులు)
కొండ మన్నెమరాజు కోట కేతుండు (కల్లు ప్రతిష్ఠ కథ **1423** పంక్తులు)
ఒక వేయు అశ్వాల నొనర ప్రతాప
రుద్రుడు పంపించె రూఢ సంగతిని (కల్లు ప్రతిష్ఠ కథ - **1455 - 1456** పంక్తులు)
Pingali Laxmikantham, op. cit., pp. 281, 292, 293.

33. The research findings of Umakantham, Virabhdra Rao, Mallampalli Soma Sekhara Sharma, Pingali Laxmikantham confirm that the Battle of Palanadu took place in the year 1181 or 1182 A.D.

34. Nagaiah, G., **Telugu Sahitya Samiksha**, Vol. II, Tirupathi 1985, p. 385.

35. See appendix-VI

36. Yashoda Devi.Varanasi , History of Andhra country 1000 A.D. to 1150 A.D. subsidiary dynasties, J.A.H.R.S. vol. XXIII, July, 1954 to April, 1956, p. 13.

37. Kodanda Ramaiah. Timmawajjala , Katamaraju katha **Bharathi**, Telugu, may 1953, p. 435.

38. Prabhakara Sastri. Veturi , (ed) : **Katamaraju katha**, Madras 1953, p. xxix.

39. Subba Rao, T., in his comprehensive work on Katawaraju refers to fix the date somewhere between 1267 and 1297. He supports the argument of Devulapalli Venkata Krishna Rao who identified date of the war as 17-03-1282.
Subba Rao, T., *op. cit.*, p. cvi.

40. Saka Samvatsara.

41. Mohan Rao, K , the History of Katamaraju and his times based on palm-leaf manuscripts, unpublished Ph.D. thesis, Osmania University, 1990, pp. 161 - 165.

42. Mohan Rao, K , op-cit. p. 162.
43. Chaitra Shudha Dasami
44. Vadarupa Maddulati kavi : Avula Valuraju katha
Mallaiah : Pampadri katha
Kanaka Bandi Gattaiah : Avula Poluraju katha
Gangula Pina Yellaiah : Kariyavula Raju katha
Katte Boyina Maraiah : Katamaraju patnam kattina katha
Venkatadri : Papanuka katha
Jarugupelli Chennaiah : Agumanchi katha
45. Swami Kanna Pillai, **Indian Ephemeris** A.D. 700 to A.D. 1799, Madras, 1922, p. 328
46. Different arguments are made on the authenticity of this inscription by various scholars.
47. For details, see, A. Chandrasekhar, **Fairs and festivals Nellore District**, Andhra Pradesh, 1961, pp. 106 to 107.
48. We come across a number of rulers by name Nallasiddi in Nellore region from 8th to 13th century. Some of them belonged to the family of Pallavas of Kanchi who fled to this region on account of the pressure from the Cholas. Even among the Telugu Chodas who had come from the Chola country, we find the name of Nallasiddi. The one with whom Katamaraju entered into an agreement might be the Telugu Chola Nallasiddi who was ruling Nellore region around 1159 A.D. according to Dongalasani inscription. This Nallasiddi was a contemporary of Kakati Rudradeva (1158-1195) who was also known as Pratapa Rudra-I confirming the Gundlapalem inscription. 'Pratapa' was a common title to many of the medieval chiefs denoting their valour.
49. A number of suggestions were made by earlier scholars to fix the date by either ignoring or doubting the accuracy of the oral narratives. But the above date meets all the requirements of oral narratives which are unanimous in expressing the date on the traditional lines.
Swamy Kannu Pillai, **An Indian Ephemeris**, vol.III, Madras, 1922, p.328.
50. Wife of Nallasiddi, however some kaifiyats mentioned her as sister of Nallasiddi who was not aware of the ***Pullari*** agreement between Nallasiddi and Katamaraju. She objected to the grazing of cattle in her land and instigated Boyas to kill the cattle of Yadavas.

6

Conclusion

India is the richest treasure house of ancient knowledge handed down to us through generations from times immemorial. The knowledge is preserved for long in the oral tradition. Our ancients have developed unfailing techniques for the preservation of this knowledge. They intended that the knowledge should be disseminated in such a way that the low and the high in the society could have a free access to at least the essence of it. Thus, the *Marga* tradition is meant for the elite sections and *Desi* tradition is designed for the masses. While the *Marga* tradition adopted Sanskrit language, grammar, prosody metre etc., the *Desi* tradition is developed with the local language, metre, rhythm and so on. These structures are proved to be fool proof in transmitting the knowledge in a fixed narrative form. They depended solely on collective human memory in preservation and transmission of the knowledge. As the society became complex in later times and that each one had to play a specific role, a few families had to be entrusted to serve the society as the treasure-houses of different branches of knowledge. Since knowledge grew enormously with the contributions of generation after generation to it, it had to be branched off and these branches had to be entrusted to different families who took this onorous responsibility of preserving their respective branches of knowledge upon themselves. Thus, the ancient knowledge, the Veda, has been primarily classified into four branches and later each branch has been further divided into different sub-branches. Because of the voluminous growth of these branches at various regions in India, the regional variations have also entered into a particular branch. As these branches and regional variations had increased in number, the number of families who were entrusted with a particular branch of knowledge had also increased. While the basic knowledge is in the Rik form, its applications have taken the form of *Yajus (Mantra)* and *Sama* (in musical notations). In *Atharvana* we have the combination of the *Mantra* and the *Tantra* including the basic sciences like Ayurveda. When this knowledge has been systematised and rendered in an orderly form, the same knowledge has been presented in a different form, namely the Puranas by the same author, sage Vedavyasa. These Puranas are designed as encyclopaedias which touch upon the essentials of every branch of knowledge, secular, religious and spiritual. The Puranas transmit this knowledge through a number of episodes to create interest in the common man. No distinction is made and no qualifications were prescribed to acquire this knowledge. But the study of the Veda and Sastras require rigorous training under a *Guru* or a Master or a teacher.

The Puranas have also grown in number with the addition of eighteen more Upapuranas to the original eighteen Mahapuranas which were composed in the later times. Each Mahapurana provides us with the knowledge of five major areas known as *Pancha Lakshanas* in the Puranic terminology. One of these five major areas is the history of royal families and their genealogies known as *Vamshanu charitam.* Now we have different kinds of Puranas and the knowledge has been disseminated among the different sections of the society and also different regions of the country.

The *Sthalapuranas* speak of the significance and the history of the places or *Kshetras.* The village, the temple, the *Kshetras,* the rivers, the mountains have thus gained popularity through their own Puranas which depict their history and religious or spiritual or commercial significance.

In the same way, the society has grown enormously in size . With the growth of civilization, numerous occupations have come into existence and the families which pursued different occupations have slowly been fossilised into castes in course of time. With these developments *Kulapuranas* have come into existence. These *Kulapuranas* explain the origin of the occupation and try to trace the founders of these occupations to be the direct descendents of that primordial couple Siva and Parvathi. Thus, each *Kula* claims its origin from that original source and thus, established their equal social status in relation to other communities. The *Kulapuranas* also established a sense of pride and satisfaction among the members of their community and they took sufficient care to wipe out the inferiority complex syndrome from those who pursue an occupation. No occupation is considered high or low by the society because each one is given a very important role to play in the economic front of the society and also the religious rituals and ceremonies of every family. Each family irrespective of his socio-economic and political status in the society has to depend and take services from every other community. These *Kulapuranas* even claim that their participation was indispensable in the marriage ceremony of that primordial couple Parvathi and Siva. A Hindu individual irrespective of his caste is supposed to undergo sixteen *samskaras (Sodasa samskaras)* starting from his entry into his mother's womb to his obsequies. In some of these *Samskaras,* particularly at the time of marriage and the last rites, the co-operation is sought from people of many castes including Medaras (Bamboo cutters and mat makers), Kummaras (Pot makers), Rajakas (Washermen) etc. Thus, the ancient society though complex was integrated into one due to mutual dependence in all social, cultural and economic activities in the larger societal existence.

Besides these Puranas, ancient classical literature consists of two great epics, the Ramayana and the Mahabharatha which are histories of two great royal lines of ancient India. Along with the Mahapuranas these epics have also become very popular among the common people. They are the histories of two or three important generations of two major dynasties of different *Yugas,* both culminating into great battles between the evil and the good resulting in the ultimate victory of good over evil. These epics have become the subjects of a number of literary and art form which were designed to entertain common man. Besides the biographical accounts, these epics also explain the essence of the *Dharma* and the knowledge of the ancients. Thus, the entertainment of the people high and low had a noble purpose of educating the people to follow the right path. On these lines each community has also been keeping its history and culture preserved in folk literary form and entrusted this job of preservation and propagation to a special branch of their community. The significant events, their family histories form part of their narration which give the community a sense of pride and self respect. Thus, a new sub-branch has emerged within the major occupational caste. We may not be able to trace the origin of these sub-castes in a fixed time frame but the development of vernaculars like Telugu which acquired the status of the standard literature by 10th and 11th century give us a clue to trace the origin of the Telugu folk literary forms and narratives, simultaneously with the elitist Telugu literature. The presently available folk literature has developed during the past one thousand years.

While knowledge in the form of Scriptures, Sastras, Sutras etc., adopted higher language techniques by grammar, metre, prosody, *swara* etc., the narratives meant for the common man adopted various attractive forms which include audio-visuals like music, dance, paintings and theatric arts. The Puranas were also considered as useful and purposeful oral narratives as they imparted education with entertainment. The various kinds of Puranas were written and propagated for building up a social order and to discipline every constituent member of the society irrespective of caste and creed. The ancient literature both *Marga* and *Desi* have served the twin objectives of the evolution of soul and the preservation of social order based on *Dharma* which is secular. The *Kulapuranas* stress the importance of pursuing one's own occupation, *Kulavrutti,* with identity, dignity and pride rather than accepting a hierarchical and compulsive social structure and divisive stratification in the present parlance of understanding the Indian caste system. The exclusivity of a caste in respect of the traditional occupation is mainly stressed by the Puranas to avoid confusion and to remove competition from other communities. Thus, the caste system provided employment to every person without contempt and competition among various groups of artisans, traders, cultivators etc. As an attempt to preserve this exclusivity and work for all, the special narratives designed for each community have also undergone changes from time to time, in content, language, literary textual form and the techniques of presentation. In this light, the available Telugu folk literature in the forms which are in vogue today have come into existence since the beginning of the last millennium.

For the preservation of oral texts intact in their original form and content, the ancients have entrusted the job to some families within their communities as their sole activity to serve the community. The community has taken up the responsibility of maintaining such families not as a compulsion but as a sacred duty of all the members of the community. They made no distinction between the Veda or a *Kulapurana* for this purpose. Each 'genre' is considered the most important one for that particular community to patronise. Therefore, the few families who were entrusted with the job of preservation of the ancient knowledge or the history of a family were considered a special class of its own within the community who should not take up any other job or involve themselves in any activity other than what was entrusted to them. Infact, this was a great sacrifice on the part of such families who took up such an onerous responsibility. In the beginning, they were respected but as the time passed, they were patronised as a compulsion. Since the traditional occupations have almost dissappeared today, such people are being treated as nuisance and they are degraded to the level of caste beggars or lazy nomads. What little we could learn about the remote past through this folk literature is the sole contribution of these families who preserved and transmitted the knowledge and information through the generations. These nomadic tribes are the custodians of the family genealogies, history, culture and the recorders of great events and builders of the image and pride of their community by narrating the heroic deeds of the great personalities of their community in the historic times.

The narratives of these sub-sects can be classified into two major parts. The first part is legendary accounts of the hoary past tracing the origin of their community or occupation, namely service and artisan castes to the beginning of this Universe which is known as the *Srushti* (Creation) and *Prathisrushti* (Pro creation), the two major characteristics of any *Mahapurana.* Some of the castes claim their origin along with the *Srushti,* the creation of Universe and some others claim that they came into existence in response to the arising needs of society in course of time. This legendary part also includes the origin of the entertaining folk as a sub-caste within the *caste organisation in a later time. These Kulapuranas are like Sthalapuranas* which trace their origin to the remote past and ascribe great antiquity to the emergence of occupational groups and the emergence of caste system. In this attempt, the founders of the castes are claimed to be either the descendants or children of and are created out of sweat or hairlock etc., of great divinities or as constituent part of the whole phenomena of the Creation or the descendants or children of sages (Bhavana and Markandeya) or the divine personalities (Vishwakarma). Thus, their claim of great antiquity and connection with the primordial forces gave them the necessary legitimisation and ascribed respectability to their occupation and sense of dignity of labour to the pursuants of such occupations. Thus, all the occupational castes and along with their depandant sub-castes have acquired unquestionable sanctity. The narratives further claim that even the tools of some artisans were handed down to them from the divine source. In the case of potters, it is said that the technology of baked pot making has also had the divine origin. Thus, various occupations, the necessary skills and tools have been ascribed respectability and it is thus evident that these occupations were never considered by the ancients as mean or low in any respect.

The Mahapuranas give a very clear account of the origin of various species as having born from the only source i.e. Prajapathi. Thus, the human specie is also born along with other species to the same Prajapathi. So the human species cannot claim a superior status to other species with regard to their birth, because all the species have originated from the same source. The Puranas only emphasise the fact that men in general have more responsibilities and duties since they are endowed with intellect to choose between good and bad unlike other species which depend only on instinct. A child has to be reared properly to grow into a responsible member of society whether he chooses to adopt worldly life or spiritual life. Man has, thus, an open access to the knowledge-worldliness and spirituality. Therefore, every child is initiated into 'human' life by opening the inner 'eye' (*Upa-nayana*) with which he can shed away the animal phase of his life. Thus, the initiation into learning the skills both temporal and spiritual is considered as a second birth and the initiated person is called the *dwiza* (twice born). This new 'eye' opens to him new vistas for acquiring either professional skills or occupational skills or spiritual or scriptural knowledge. None of these branches of knowledge is considered superior to the other. The *Kulapuranas* treat the knowledge contained in the philosophical, scientific and technological contents with equal regard. As a mark of acquiring this new insight every learner is blessed with the sacred thread worn across his chest, known as *Jandyam*. Many of these occupational castes still wear this sacred thread. Thus, no caste could claim and exclusive right for acquiring knowledge in the ancient times. The Puranas donot ascribe any exclusivity to any particular caste whether high or low. The caste system, in the modern parlance of Management, is an organisational structure of the society and various people pursued different occupations as part of this mighty structure. No Purana including these *Kulapuranas* mention any preferences or undue privileges or discrimination shown towards any particular community.

The second part of their narratives include the great events and the lives of great heroes belonging to their community which establish their personal pride, prestige, self-respect and dignity in the seemingly complex system of a stratified society. The great events include some great battles fought by these communities to defend their honour such as the battle of Erragaddapadu (1163 A.D) in which Katamaraju, the hero of the Yadava community heroically fought against Nallasiddi, the king of Nellore Mandala and the Battle of Palnad (1182 A.D.) which was a heroic war between two half brothers for the kingdom of Palnad which resembled the great battle of the Mahabharatha in its miniature form. In another incident the

Vaisya community strongly protested the proposal of a king belonging to Eastern Chalukya or Chalukya Chola line by name Vishnuvardhana to marry Kanyaka, a beautiful girl of Vaisya community. The Vaisya community declined this matrimonial offer from their king. When the king wanted to impose his desire and marched into the village with a military force, the entire community had immolated themselves to save their honour. This incident established that the family honour could not be compromised upon under any circumstance. In another instance an ordinary Madivelu Machaiah, a washerman, had fought against the great army of King Bijjala who tried to force him to wash King's clothes against his will. Madivelu Machaiah won the war with his supernatural power as he was a great devotee of Lord Siva. King Bijjala might have been a follower of Jainism. Perhaps this incident might belong to the times when Virasaivism was on the rise under Basava, a minister of King Bijjala.

Some of the entertaining folk have also traced their origin during the early medieval times. In many such cases the origin of the sub-caste is ascribed to the marriages between men belonging to a higher caste and women belonging to a lower caste (*Anuloma*) or illicit relation. In some cases those who are declared as outcastes for their questionable behaviour have later been excused and tolerated as a dependant sub-caste who are assigned the job of maintaining genealogies of various families of the community. Thus, each major caste right from the Braḥmins down to the lowest in the hierarchical structure of caste system have been patronising one or more than one sub-castes to be solely dependant on their respective major communities. These sub-castes would periodically visit various villages in our state wherever they find their patron community lives in a sizeable number and collect donations from them. When they enter the village they announce their arrival to the elders or the leader of the patron-community and then visit other households to remind them of their family pedigree. Generally they visit these villages after the closer of the agricultural operations for the season. As decided by the elders of the community their teams would exhibit their art and entertain their folk. These teams carry with them the copper plate grants issued in the name of the chief deity of the community to claim their demand with unshakable legitimacy. Generally the community entertains no doubts about the authenticity of their claim. The community house holds do not fail to pay their contributions and usual gifts to these entertaining teams.

The entertaining sub-caste of a community is further divided into few teams or groups who are granted *Mirasi.* These goups are very strictly attached themselves only to those *Mirasi* villages to which they belong. They seldom visit the *Mirasis* of other groups within their sub-castes. Even if they have to go to some village which does not fall in their *Mirasi,* on account of any other work, they refrain from exhibiting their art even as a sample in such villages. Thus, these groups have great respect for the rights of other groups and feel contended with what they are granted. They confine themselves to their own respective jurisdictional areas. Another great characteristic of these sub-castes is that they do not accept any contribution from any other community even with in their own jurisdiction though they exhibit their art in open place where all are welcome to witness the performance. They prefer to live a simple life and move from village to village with their entire entourage. Since they are always on their move with no fixed occupation for themselves other than the folk performances, they choose to live in their native villages for a short period once in two or three years when they are not visiting their *Mirasi* villages. They have no settled life and so called nomadic tribes. Infact they cannot be called 'nomads' in the technical sense of the word because they donot move out of their jurisdictional area and also claim their nativity to a specific part of the region. However, their dependance on the major community for their livelihood continued from generation to generation. These sub-castes, though in later times came to be considered inferior to the main caste, do not suffer from inferiority complex. They feel that they are serving the community for a noble purpose and the community in turn shows its regard to them as their well-wishers.

Most distressing fact with regard to the social status of these sub-castes in the recent times is that even an untouchable community it self, treates its own sub-caste as untouchables to them (Dakkalis). While the society was not based on cash economy till the establishment of the English rule in India, these sub-castes used to get their livelihood directly from these patron-communities in kind. As long as the payment in kind was in vouge, the economic inequality was absent and the social affinity between the caste and the intracaste was stronger. The English government has transformed the rural economy into market economy through various reforms. The land is made a commodity in the modern sense to be bought and sold. The development of land market coupled with the commercialisation of agriculture resulted in an unhealthy competition among those who are engaged in agricultural operation and also those service and artisan castes who depend on agriculture for their livelihood. The decline of traditional croping pattern and the native handy crafts during the British rule had shattered the stable rural economy. The sub-castes are being treated as the parasite class or a begging caste. This degradation of various social and cultural groups has culminated in marginalising them from the main stream of the social fabric by the end of the British rule. The studies undertaken by the British have grouped these entertaining folks as dependent castes and also treated them as thiefs and criminal communities. However, these communities still retain their self respect and pride. But the present castes have abandoned their traditional artisan and service occupations and adopted modern ways of living. Now the entire economy has transformed into cash economy and the services and goods are available only on cash payments. The rise of consumerism has further aggravated the system and in place of caste system casteism has grown in the modern times. Along with their major castes, the sub-castes are also forced to adopt themselves to the changing economic scenario and now any dependence on any one in any form is being despised.

These nomadic sub-castes which are attatched to their respective main castes have adopted the art forms, both folk and classical, to present the history and the genealogies of their respective castes. Their narratives adopted the structure and contents of the Mahapuranas. Surprisingly the lowest of the low

(Dakkali and Chindu) sub-castes narrates the *Jambavapurana* which explains the Creation of the Universe and the evolution and transmigration of a soul as a typical Mahapurana. Their language and style of presentation appears to be classical in its art. The dramatic episodes like *Satisavitri, Krishnarjunayuddam, Virabhimanya, Satya Harichandra* etc., do not differ in its content from the major Puranas. The other sub-castes of higher castes as per their placement upwards in the social hierarchy appear to have adopted the Puranic narrative form while they drew less and less content from the classical Puranas, as they go up. These sub-castes have mainly took to give a respectable place to their occupation and their occupational skills by tracing their origin to the pri-mordial phase. The Pandavulavaru narrate the stories from the Mahabharatha, *Yayathicharitra* and *Pandavavanavasamu* while the Runzas attatched to Vishwabrahmins narrate *Parvathikalyanam.* The Viramustis attached to Vaisyas narrate *Vasavi Kanyaka Parameshwari Katha* and the Vipravinodis attached to Brahmins do not narrate any Puranas but they perform only magic shows to entertain their patrons. Bhatrazus belonging to Kshatriya community would only read out the genealogies and *Gotras* of their patron community. Thus, the narratives of these sub-castes had no need to draw much from the classical literature, because the higher castes in the social hierarchy were already exposed to the traditional and classical literature and as such there was no need to depend on their respective sub-castes for this purpose. This would reveal that the ancients paid considerable attention in passing on the knowledge of the Puranic wisdom to the lowest in the social hierarchy. They were taught the essense of the Puranic wisdom through more attractive dramatic art forms, because these communities cannot acquire the knowledge of traditional knowledge by themselves. These communities which can acquire this knowledge on their own were only maintaining their sub-caste for the preservation of their family histories and genealogies. The Brahmins do not generally need any body to remind them of their *Gotra* and family pedigree. Therefore, they would only maintain the Vipravinodis for entertaining them with magic shows.

Almost all these sub-castes have their narratives written on palm-leaves from time to time. These palm-leaf manuscripts are copied for handing down to the new teams from generation after generation. Each team will have a copy of their narrative inscribed on palm-leaves which is carried with them wherever they go for the performance. Some such manuscripts written some two or three centuries before are preserved in Oriental Manuscripts Libraries of Madras and Tirupati. These are very important sources for research in the area of folk studies. Surprisingly, the literary texts of these narratives are composed in *Dwipada Manjeera* metre in Telugu. The *Dwipada kavyas* appear in Telugu literature from about 11th and 12th centruries. But *Dwipada Manjeera* metre was also videly used in the earlier times in Andhradesa. The narratives of lower sub-castes have adopted the *Dwipada* form of Telugu literature of elite sections. Since lower sub-castes are illiterate, they got by heart the texts for presentation. Though they carry the manuscripts with them they cannot read the texts. But they can recite these texts without a flaw in either the content or the pronunciation. The sub-castes from Runzas and above can read and write but they are not very particular to develop and preserve the manuscripts because their narratives do not draw much content from the traditional literature. This reveals that the elite writers have composed the literary texts and trained the illiterate lower sub-caste to recite these texts to their respective communities. Thus, the ancients appear to have taken care in providing proper education to the lowest strata of the society who were illiterate. These sub-castes recite their respective Puranas in the Telugu language of the elite during their performances but they switch back to their dialect in their normal conservation. This would tell us the fact that they were trained initially by the elite section and later their children learnt the recitation from the elders of their community. This is also evident in the fact that the performing art forms like *Yakshaganas, Bhamakalapam* etc., are taught by the schalors-cum-performing artists of the elite sections to the other communities in the medieval times. These classical-cum-folk art forms have been also adopted by the lower sub-castes to entertain their respective communities. Thus, there is a dynamic interaction between the elite and the other communities in the adaptation and standardisation of their respective performing arts. The art has, thus, become one of the main integrating factors of the society.

Numerous castes and sub-castes projecting a multifaceted social structure within the general frame work in the society ascribe to it apparently a heterogeneity in character. The ancient Hindu society facilitated the development of each caste in its prescribed path for generations without giving a scope for internal competition. Each caste group has developed as an independent unit with its own Puranic legends, folk art, trade, marriage regulations, interpersonal relationship, customs, family traditions, *Kulapanchayats,* occupational regulations etc. We do not find any intercaste interference in these matters which are purely concerning the particular caste. Even the State used to maintain non-interference in the customary matters of the caste. The judgements or *thirmanas of Kulapanchayats* or the elders of their respective communities were considered final in these respects. No appeals were preferred even in the King's court. Thus, each caste with its distinct culture, art, customs, traditions, occupations has grown into a self reliant functional unit of a broad spectrum. But a closer examination of the working of these units, though numerous in number and complex in their structures, would reveal that there was an indispensable interdependence among all the communities on social, religious and economic fronts. The religions of the historical period till the spread of Islam and Christianity in India namely Jainism, Buddhism, Advaitam, Dvaitam, Visistadvaitam, Shakticult, Bhakticult etc., have cut across the various caste communities within the Hindu fold. Similarly the *Samskaras* and the important rituals, festivals, pilgrimages, social values, life styles, ornaments, dress and in all matters of day-to-day routine, no distinction was made between one caste and the other barring some minor variations in rituals and practices. Certain families' specific rituals and customary practices also look different from the other families with in the same community. But it cannot be viewed as a factor of disintegrity.

On the lines of the Mahapuranas, the numerous *Kulapuranas* recited by the sub-castes from top to the lowest of the low in the social hierarchy can be classified into four groups representing the four main religions of Hindu culture, namely the Saiva, Vaishnava, Brahma and Shakta. But Saiva and Shakta religions appear to be more dominant. While Saivism added philosophical content, Shakta contributed ritual content to their religious practices. The Shakta has provided for numerous minor goddesses to be worshipped by the different communities and in different localities. But, however, these minor goddesses or gods were shown mostly as the offsprings of the primordial couple Siva and Parvathi of emerging directly from the un manifest Brahma. Therefore, the worship of numerous gods and goddesses had not caused any divisiveness or mutual hatred or rivalry among them. The folklore does not show any dissent in the matter of religious practices of these numerous communities. On the other hand, they showed mutual respect and understanding of various religious practices and beliefs and tried to establish the 'Oneness' of the Ultimate Reality which is the source of all Creation. Thus, the folklore of these nomadic tribes firmly established and promoted the unity of Hindu culture with mutually respecting different religious beliefs and practices within its fold.

Each family might be interested in establishing its own identity in its own community with a claim to excellence either in their occupational skills or values of living and appreciable character. It may be viewed as a healthy competition and a positive development among the various families to excel one another in noble qualities and vying with each other in self-respect. Similarly each caste group also wanted to establish its relevance, importance and indispensability in the functioning of the society as a whole. Thus, the main castes depended on their respective sub-castes to articulate their social relevance and constructive participation. The collective endeavor of the society to promote cultural unity and social harmony bore the desirable fruit for which all the main castes played their roles as complementary units while the articulating sub-castes played the role of supplementaries through the preservation and propagation of their respective 'little' traditions as sub-units of a pan-Indian culture. Though these sub-castes depend on their respective major castes for their livelihood, it may be said that the major caste communities, infact, depended more on their respective sub-castes to speak for their communities. Till the coming of Europeans, these castes and sub-castes were intervowen to make a well decorated social fabric with an underlying unity, integrity and homogeneity at their core.

APPENDIX - I

The list of Nomadic Tribes attached to each major caste under Varna system

Sl. No.	*Caste*		*Nomadic Tribes*
1.	Brahmins		: Vipravinodis
2.	Kshatriyas		: Bhatrajus
3.	Vaisyas		: Viramustis
4.	Sudras :		
	a.	**Agriculture castes**	
	(i)	Kapu, Kamma and Reddys	: Pichikuntlas
	(ii)	Gollas	: Mandahechus
	b.	**Artisan castes**	
	(i)	Padmasalis	(i) Sadana Surulu
			(ii) Kunapuli varu
	(iii)	Vishwabrahmins	(i) Runzas
			(ii) Panasas
	(iii)	Kummaras (Potters)	Pekkara, or Kulam Biddalu
	c.	**Service castes**	
	(i)	Rajakas (Washer men)	(i) Patamu varu
			(ii) Ganjikuti varu
	(ii)	Mangalis (Barber)	Addapusingas
	d.	**Other castes**	
	(i)	Mutrasi or Tenugus	(i) Pandavula varu
	(ii)	Kakipadigela varu	

(ii) Goudas	(i) Goudajettis (ii) Enuti varu
(iii) Madigas	(i) Chindu Bhagothula varu (ii) Dakkalis
(iv) Medaras	Adikodukulu
(v) Malas	(i) Gurram malalu (ii) Malamasti

APPENDIX - II
Copper Plate of the Mandahechus

వుందేచ్చుల తామ్రపత్రవు

శ్రీ॥ స్వస్తి సమస్త శాలివాహన శత వరు 9లు 1465 యేండ్లగు చాంద్రమాన ఈశ్వర నామ సంవత్సర శ్రావణ శు. 5 గురువారం నాడు శ్రీ బిత్తల పాటు నూకమాంబ కంచిలో మహాదేవుని ముఖమంటపాన ప్రప్పరన్నకు యాదవుడు చిత్తుడు పల్లకొండ కాటమరాజు వజ్ర సింహాసనారుడు తెక్కూచు నద్రి పులి చర్మ దేవయ్య భూతనాధుడైన భత్తునికి వుదరి జనహువంటు ధర్మశాసన పత్రిక ప్రశమమహేమయా వినాధ అష్టాంగయోగ ఆయురాద్రంత్తి ప్రధాన పర తువ్వరకు కుటాపరమహషాసుర శుంభని శుంభ మహారాక్షస శిఖర ఖండన దూంమ్రలోచన త్రిపుర రాక్షస సంహ్మారకారణాలి వర్ధ విడుకాంది పాలినాంత్రి లాణ / పైను గుంచి పాలు మధిరె స్తంబాత్ర్యిలలే రడకాండ / బెల్ల కాండ / రాజ కాండ / పొదిలే / మధిరే / నెల్లూరు / గాదారరం మొదలిన నానా రాజ్యాల కులం గోత్రవారి పంపున / బొలా అయితము రాజు యిచ్చిన ధర్మశాసన పత్రికె / పురుగంటును / నామంత్రి రాగలకు ఓగడంపరిలెను / పోరుగంటు శెటుడెకంద్యల మకంచికి అయితము రాజు గాం 79 వలెటువాని 9 ఉభయరాజుల గూర్చి పంపినాను పద్మ రాధకులున్ను - ఆయాది పురపరాది శురులున్ను స్వస్తి సమస్త నిజమాంక మార్థిక ప్రశస్త సమీతులయిన మూడు దిక్కులపైన పెద్ద అయినా పలవారున్ను - పృదివి 56 రు దేశాలవారున్ను - దేవగిరి మనలమునా మూల సమస్త యెన పెక్కంద్రు వీర పరివారములును / సకల సామ్యవంతులున్ను శెయిగత్తులున్ను / బలవాదులయిన శీల వాదున్ను / యల్ల గొర్ల శింహ్యాన్ను స్వామి కార్య దురందరులున్ను / సలదనమ్య వంతులున్ను / పరశాణసహైదరోలున్ను / శ్రీకృష్ణరాయుని నిజమూల భృత్యులయి శ్రీమతువురు గంటను కో అవిదు / కొండవల్లి / వెనుకంబపోలు / నల్లగోడ / దెవకోడ - వరిశ - రావకొండ / వెకుదల యనవానా రాజ్యాల బడుగుల వారు / యిచ్చిన పత్రికే బడుగుల వారున్ను

విరుల వారున్ను / మీలోను బరుదాన చల్లును / చల్లదని కంచిలో పల్లి యాభయి ఆరు దేశాల / పెకంఁడ్రల మనము ఖానకు వస్తెను / మీ మాటలు విన పంబాయ గాను సభా అఁత్రుసు కూభకంనపుడు మీ మాటలు పెకంఁడ్రు విని పూర్వ మరిమానులున్ను / పేరామరిశ చెశిమోగిశిన పెలసు / విరుల వారుతాలరి పోయినంతలోను / శాపనాలంగల బిరుదావర మెమ పర్యామరి శచెరి/ కుమవసత్త మున్ను / గరుడ పరిగెలున్ను / హనువంత పతిగెలున్ను ఆలపద్నులున్ను / శంబులు విరణాలున్ను / శ్రీరామ మాడలున్ను / నామంతి రాగలున్ను / బసువటెంకపు పతిలున్ను / చులు విచెలున్ను / జగడం గొడుగులున్ను / ఔలరేగలున్ను / ముత్యాల షరాలున్ను / చిఁత్రి గోరుగులున్ను / వింజామరలున్ను / శ్రీ రామ శలగలున్ను వీణ వేణునాధములున్ను మడుమపురి శంకులున్ను / మొక ముఖి రుఁద్రాక్షలున్ను భల్లాణుటెక్క్యములున్ను / బసవశంకర చిరుదులున్ను / సంగధితోరణాలున్ను / చాయ చాయ గొల్లేండ్లున్ను / నవసందుల గొల్లేండ్లున్ను / బల్లణు దట్టీలున్ను పటుపతావల్లున్ను / ఘంటల వతాణుంబులున్ను / తమ మతమున్ను / విరణాలున్ను / పంబలు కాలేలున్ను / కైమారలున్ను / ఘంటల వతాణుంబులున్ను / తమ మతమున్ను విరణాలున్ను / పంబలు కాలేలున్ను / కైమారలున్ను / హిశ్యరునికెన్ని / ఁశమకూ విష్ణుకు గల బిరుదల్లు యాదవులు కుచేల్లున్ను / యె 72 నియోగులు కలవని గెలిచ వచ్చినందుకు సుట్లు పెకంఁడ్రిలు మొదలయిన కులం వారిని కూచుఁక్రోని విచారించి ఓరుగంటు ఁప్రతాపరుఁద్రుదున్ను / నాలు జోజులున్ పుల్లేడ పెగిం చల్లంచూరు // కంచికరు కల్యాణ నుసష ముఖ్యమైన శుభశాభనాని పృదివింగల రాజులున్ను యీ శాసన పఁత్రికలో వాసిన బిరుదులున్ను / ము 56 దేశముల వారును సకలమైన తిదక్నిదులలోచలును / గానా వైభవములు వెరసి పూరెఁద్రియ బరదా వర్ధి వెగించెలుందుకు మందహెచ్చు భత్తునికి తగను / పన్నెంఁడ్రు గొల్లకులాలకు తగును యఁర్రగొల్ల / వునాటుగొల్ల / సజనపుగొల్ల / ముదుటవు గొల్ల / పాకనాటి గొల్ల / పెరవటు గొల్ల / ఆలగొల్ల / కరుణ గొల్ల / వెయ్య గొల్ల / నల్ల గొల్ల / ముష్టి గొల్ల / వకారి గొల్ల / పన్నెండు కులాలకు ఎఁర్రగొల్ల ముల్లంత యచ్చు / పరిముల్లంత

మగు / విభూతి విరిగొందానికి అందారుకతలు పన్నెండు గొల్ల కులాలకు మందేచ్చు భత్తునికి తగును / యితని యేడు ఆవులుగల గొల్ల ఆవు నగయు వశలదే / 2 మేకలు ముల్లుకత్తి గల గొర్రెపిల్ల యెకనుయివ గలరు వయవసాయం చేసే గొల్ల పచ్చడ్డం యివ్వవలెను / యెరువురకబం పోతనం చేసిన పశువుల ఆకచిన యాడి జీతం యివ్వగలరు నెల / యిక్రమున సకల దేశాల వారున్ను అన్నపానాదులు పెట్టి తిప్ప సంతోషం బోసనయు హమస్నినతాబి మందహెచ్చుబత్తునికి యిచెది / యి ధర్మము తప్పరాదు అంల్లంవుల్లనైన భారంకు చెదైన నడిపించెడి / నడవని వారు పిత్రుమాత్రులకు తప్పిన వారు శ్రీ కంచి కాశి కల్యాణనందో కాండ మొదలయిన కంచి పహ్మాపు పెదలున్ను / కపడిచెపత్తమి / యివ్వని వారికి కాని లోగో మాత్య బ్రహ్మత్య పాతకంశిదించును / శ్రీ భమస్తు స్పత్తాద్రి గుణం పుణ్యం పరవత్తాను పాలనం / పరదలోప హారణ్య స్పదత నిష్ట లంభవతు యిధర్మ శాసనం విన్నవార్కి సదివిన వార్కి వ్రాసిన వార్కి పుణ్యంలుగును / ధర్మపాలన యోర్మ వ్యే దానా క్షమోను పాలనందోశస్యశ యువాప్నతి పాలనందక్షన పదం // శ్రీ శ్రీం జెయునూ / శ్రీరామా శ్రీ శితా రామా శ్రీ జయరా / యా -

APPENDIX - III

The Genealogical Table of Eastern Chalukyas

- Kubja Vishnuvardhana (624-641 A.D)
  - Jayasimhavallabha-I (641-673 A.D.)
  - Indrabhattaraka (673 A.D.)
    - Vishnuvardhana-II (673-681 A.D.)
      - Mangi Yuvaraju (681-705 A.D.)
        - Jayasimha-II (705-718 A.D.)
        - Vishnuvardhana-III (718-752 A.D.)
          - Vijayaditya-I (752-771 A.D.)
            - Vishnuvardhana-IV (771-806 A.D.)
        - Kokkali - Vikramaditya (705 A.D.)
          - Mangi Yuvaraju-II (Madhya Kalinga)

Narendramrugaraja Vijayaditya (806-846 A.D.)

Bhimasaluki

Shilamahadevi (Rashtrakutadruva)

Indra

Shilamahadevi

Kalivishnuvardhana (846-848 A.D.)

Gunaga Vijayaditya-III (848-892 A.D.)

Vikramaditya Yuvaraja

Chalukyabhima-I (892-921 A.D.)

Nrupakama

Yudhamalla-I

Tala-I (928 A.D.)

Yuddhamallu-II (928-935 A.D)

Talaraju-II

Badavaraju

Vikramaditya-II (928-935 A.D.)

Kollabhiganda-Vijayaditya-IV (921 A.D.)

Ammaraju-I (921-928 A.D.)

Chalukyabhima-II (936-945 A.D.)

Ammaraju-II (945-970 A.D.)

Kundavva Arinjaya (Son of Chola Parantaka)

Kantikabheta-Bhima (936 A.D.)

Vijayaditya-V (Pitapuram) (928 A.D.)

Danarnava (970-973 A.D.)

Sundarachola

Saktivarma-I (999-1011 A.D.)

Vimaladitya (1011-1018 A.D)

Kundavva

Aditya-II

Arumoli Varman Rajarja

Vimaladitya

Rajendra-I

Vijayaditya-VI (1061-1076 A.D.)

Rajaraja Narendra (1019-1061 A.D.)

Amangadevi

Saktivarm

Sovaladevi

Rajendra Kulothunga (Founder of Chalukya Chola)

APPENDIX - IV

The Genealogical Table of Chalukya-Cholas

Kulothunga Choladeva-I
(Vishnuvardhana)
(1070-1122 A.D.)

- Rajaraja Chodagangu
- Rajaraja Mummad-ichoda
- Virachoda (Vishnuvar dhana)
- Vikramachola (1118-1135 A.D.)
- Others (3 rulers) Vishnuvar dhanas

Kulothunga Chodadeva-II
(1133-1150 A.D.)
|
Rajaraja-II
(1146-1173 A.D.)

Rajadiraja-II
(1663-1179 A.D)
|
Rajaraja-III
(1216-1246 A.D.)

APPENDIX - V

The Genealogical Table of Haihaya Dynasty

Chagi Betha Raju
(1103 A.D.)

↓

Virakamukudu
(1118 A.D.)

↓

Betha Raju (Birudankarudrudu)
(1128 A. D.)

↓

Anugu Raju (Kama Raju)
(1134-1140)

↓

↓	↓
Nalagama Raju (1147 A.D.)	Malideva Raju (1147 A.D.)

APPENDIX - VI

The Genealogical Tables from Lord Krishna to Katamaraju

According to T. Kodanda Ramaiah (Andhra Patrika)	*According to Kankanampadu palme-leaf manuscript (PolurajuKatha)*	*According to Gundlapalam inscription*		*According to Perikagudem Palm-leaf manuscipt (Jannivada Katha)*	*According to Govula Nageswara (Peddiraju) Natakam)*
1	**2**	**3**		**4**	**5**
Sri Krishna	Sri Krishna	Sri Krishna		Sri Krishna	Sri Krishna
Manmadhudu	Manmadhudu	Vijradarudu	Amrutha Gopudu	Manmadhudu	Pradummudu
Anirudrudu Indra Devudu	Ambhajudu Rayambojudu	Dadisangudu	Upanandu	Indra Devudu Ananda senudu	Aniruddrudu Vajrudu
Shagravudu	Ratnamboju		Amruthambojudu	Ambodhu	Prathibahudu
Satya	Vibhuti Bhaskarudu			Vinayambojudu	Gattambodhi Subhahudu

(Contd.)

(Contd. Appendix-VI)

According to T. Kodanda Ramaiah (Andhra Patrika)	*According to Kankanampadu palme-leaf manuscript (PolurajuKatha)*	*According to Gundlapalam inscription*	*According to Perikagudem Palm-leaf manuscipt (Jannivada Katha)*	*According to Govula Nageswara (Peddiraju) Natakam)*
1	**2**	**3**	**4**	**5**
Kuruvaludu	Jadala Shankaraiah	Kanakambojudu	Veerambodhi	Ugrasenudu
Kavulavula - Ganguraju	Virijjappa Raju	Gajayambojudu	Vijayambodhi	Sruthasenudu
Avula Valuraju	Agganala Voluraju	Rayambojudu	Rayambodhi	Upanandudu
Peddiraju	Avula Valuraju	Ratnambojudu	Chumchumbodhi	Amruthambojudu
Katamaraju [11 Generations]	Peddiraju Katamaraju [12 Generations]	Veeravijayaraju Padmanaraju Srikurmaraju	Jalambodhi Kanakambodi Yayadhri	Vijayambojudu Kanakambojudu Gajambojudu

(Contd.)

(Contd. Appendix-VI)

According to T. Kodanda Ramaiah (Andhra Patrika)	*According to Kankanampadu palme-leaf manuscript (Poluraju Katha)*	*According to Gundlapalam inscription*	*According to Perikagudem Palm-leaf manuscipt (Jannivada Katha)*	*According to Govula Nageswara (Peddiraju) Natakam)*
1	**2**	**3**	**4**	**5**
		Simhadri Raju Valluraju Peddiraju Poluraju Katamaraju [17 Generations]	Kavulavula Avula Bhupati Avula Amrutaiah Peddiraju Katamaraju [19 Generations]	Rayambojudu Ratnambojudu Padmaraju Simhadriraju Ganguraju Valaraju Peddiraju Katamaraju [23 Generations]

(Contd.)

APPENDIX - VII

List of the Respondents to the Open-ended Questionnaire Served on the Nomadic Tribes in Andhra Pradesh

Sl. No.	*Name of the Respondent*	*Age (Years)*	*Address*
I.	**Viramustis :**		
1.	Katepalli Veeraiah	60	Musharam bagh, Malakpeta, Hyderabad
2.	Kadem Yellaiah	65	-do-
3.	Ponnala Narahari	60	Chikkadaplli, Hyderabad
4.	Mittapalli Soma mallaiah	65	Shabadgoda, Hyderabad
5.	Ch. Narsimha	60	Shankarampalli, Ranga Reddy district
6.	Viramusti Hanumanthu	60	Mangalampalli, Nakrekal, Nalgonda dist.
7.	Thangedapalli Laxmaiah	70	-do-
8.	M. Pedda Veeraswamy	65	Ajampura colony, Medak district

(Contd.)

(Contd. Appendix-VII)

Sl.	*Name of the Respondents*	*Age*	*Address*
9.	M. Kamalamma	68	-do-
10.	M. Veeramma	70	-do-
11.	Karne Shiva kumar	40	Tilak Road, Kasibugga, Warangal distict
12.	Kankuri Saraiah	50	Narsampeta, Warangal district
13.	Agulla Chandramouli	50	Ghanapuram, Warangal district
14.	Mittapalli Mallaiah	60	Vardhannapeta, Warangal district
15.	Kadari Radhakrishna	50	Cherial, Warangal dist.
16.	Diviti Pochaiah	60	Dharmapuri, Karimnagar district
17.	Bonala Lingaiah	70	-do-
18.	Miriyala Appaiah	70	Burgampadu, Bhadrachalam, Khammam district
19.	Mahamkali Ramalingaiah	70	Kothagudem, Khammam district
20.	Kadem Manaiah	60	Vanaparthi, Mahaboobnagar district
21.	Sarangi Venkata Ramulu	60	Achchampeta, Mahaboobnagar, district.
22.	Miriyala Gurulingam	60	Elluru, East Godavari dist.

(Contd.)

(Contd. Appendix-VII)

Sl.	*Name of the Respondents*	*Age*	*Address*
23.	Gullapurapu Durga Rao	70	Tenali, Guntoor district
24.	K. Vijaya Prakash	45	Cheerala, Prakasham dist.
II.	**Pichikuntlas :**		
1.	Sanikommu Pothuraju	60	Banigandlapadu, Khammam district.
2.	Seelam Sivaramakoti	50	-do-
3.	Seelam Krishna	50	-do-
4.	Gaddam Ramalingam	55	Mangalapally, Narkal, Nalgonda district
5.	Nimmala Ramulu	55	Munugodu, Nalgonda dist.
6.	Pichikuntla Mallesh	45	Kalvakurthi, Mahaboobnagar district.
7.	Kanchanagalla Ramulu	60	Kandukuru, Maheshwaram, Ranga Reddy distrcit
8.	Gandam Ramulu	60	-do-
9.	Chandraiah	75	Thirumalagiripally, Ranga Reddy district
10.	Sagireddy Kulayappa	70	Ganapuram, Arlagadda,Karnool district
11.	Karneti Venkataiah	70	Darsi, Prakasham district
12.	Nimmala Seethaiah	45	Bayyaram, Garla, Khammam district.

(Contd.)

(Contd. Appedix-VII)

Sl.	*Name of the Respondents*	*Age*	*Address*
13.	Nimmala Ramulu	60	Munugodu, Nalgonda dist.
14.	Nimmala Hanumanthu	60	Bethavolu, Huzurnagar, Nalgonda district
15.	Chittibethula Narasimhulu	60	Miryalagudem, Nalgonda district
III.	**Mandahechus :**		
1.	Ura Keshavulu	55	Ellandu Village, Warangal District
2.	Ankamma	45	-do-
3.	Ilamma	45	-do-
4.	Nagamallu	55	Thorrur, Warangal District
5.	Dasaratham	55	Ammapuram, Maripeda, Warangal district
6.	Butham Narasimham	60	Datla Village, Maripeda, Warangal District
7.	Turpati Srisailam	60	-do-
8.	Peddamma	60	-do-
9.	Gangamma	40	-do-
10.	Yadagiri	60	Gurelli, Jangoan, Warangal District.
11.	Durga	30	-do-
12.	Balanarsimham	60	Choutuppal, Nalgonda District

(Contd.)

(Contd. Appendix-VII)

Sl.	*Name of the Respondents*	*Age*	*Address*
13.	Rajulu	45	Mahaboobabad, Warangal District
14.	Rajeshu	60	-do-
15.	Komuraiah	60	Shadagar, Mahaboobnagar District
16.	Parvathalu	50	-do-
17.	Komuramma	45	-do-
IV.	**Runzas :**		
1.	Brahmanatham	65	Gunaboyinapally, Nalgonda district.
2.	Bandaru Lokanatham	70	Motkuru, Nalgonda dist.
3.	Pasham Somasekharam	65	Garla, Khammam district
4.	Pasham Palalochana Rao	65	Draksharamamu, Thnuku.
5.	Geedikanti Satyanarayana	70	Rajahmundry, East Godavari district.
6.	Pasham China Somasekharam	70	Vinukonda, Guntoor dist.
V.	**Kunapulivaru :**		
1.	Bikshapathi	50	Sayampeta, Warangal dist.
2.	Puranam Venkatarajam	70	-do-
3.	Puranam Yerragattu	65	Sayampeta, Warangal dist.
4.	Kanakaiah	70	Chintagattu, Warangal district.

(Contd.)

(Contd. Appendix-VII)

Sl.	Name of the Respondents	Age	Address
5.	Narsaiah	70	-do-
6.	Kommalu	71	-do-
7.	Seetha Ramulu	75	-do-
8.	Thirupataiah	70	-do-
9.	Uppalaiah	48	-do-
10.	Ramachandram	65	Nagarjunasagar, Nalgonda district
11.	Bandaru Venugopala rao	70	Kothapeta, Vijayawada.
VI.	**Pandavula Varu :**		
1.	Yadagiri	55	Gumudelli, Jangoan, Warangal district
2.	Ramulu	60	-do-
3.	Ramaswamy	60	-do-
4.	Kistaiah	55	-do-
5.	Satyanarayana	60	-do-
6.	Saraiah	65	-do-
7.	Bikshapathi	48	-do-
8.	Narayana	58	Gumudelli, Jangoan, Warangal district
9.	Narasimha	60	Chilukalaguda, Secudrabad
10.	Gandaiah	60	-do
11.	Hanumanthu	70	-do-
12.	Manikyam	48	-do-
13.	Krishna	48	-do-
14.	Pandavula Manikyam	70	Atlapuram, Ranga Reddy district

(Contd.)

(Contd. Appendix-VII)

Sl.	*Name of the Respondents*	*Age*	*Address*
15.	Laxmaiah	60	-do-
16.	Eswaraiah	45	-do-
17.	Hanumaiah	45	-do-
18.	Agamaiah	60	Medak city, Medak dist.
VII.	**Kakipadigela Varu :**		
1.	Chikkudu Kistaiah	60	Narsampeta, Warangal district
2.	Chikkudu Govindam	55	-do-
3.	Bhadraiah	45	Narsampeta, Warangal district
4.	Poshalu	50	-do-
5.	Rangaiah	55	-do-
6.	Gopaiah	60	Ganapuram, Warangal dist.
7.	Komuraiah	60	-do-
8.	Kistaiah	65	-do-
VIII.	**Patam Chakallu :**		
1.	Induri Guru Murthy	70	Sathupally, Khammam district.
2.	Induri Kotaiah	63	Mulugu, Warangal district
3.	Turai Rajalingam	70	-do-
4.	Induri Saraiah	55	-do-
5.	Induri Krishna	50	-do-
6.	Venkata Narasimha	55	Mahaboobabad, Warangal district

(Contd.)

(Contd. Appendix-VII)

Sl.	Name of the Respondents	Age	Address
7.	Mallesham	60	Manthini, Krimnagar dist.
8.	Narsimhulu	70	Jagityal, Karimnagar dist.
9.	Siva Rao	70	-do-
10.	Rajam	50	Chettupali, Nizamabad district
11.	Patam Subba Rao	60	Bethupalli, Khammam district
IX.	**Goudajettis :**		
1.	Jetti Sammaiah	65	Chalaparthi, Narsampeta, Warangal district
2.	Seetha Ramulu	70	Jangoan, Warangal district
3.	Chandraiah	65	Malla Reddypally, Parkal, Warangal district
4.	Enuti Sammaiah	70	Palampet, Mulugu, Warangal district.
5.	Enutla Subba Rao	85	Diwanam Cheruvu, Rajahmundry
6.	Somaiah	65	Suryapeta, Nalgonda dist.
7.	Erukonda Mallaiah	70	Mahabooba bad, Warangal district
8.	Keshavulu	60	Ashwaraipalli, Warangal district

(Contd.)

(Contd. Appendix-VII)

Sl.	Name of the Respondents	Age	Address
X.	**Pekkaras :**		
1.	Eluru Suryanarayana	70	Chintalapudi village, Thirumaladevi peta, West Godavari district
2.	Satyavathi	45	-do-
3.	Medicherla Rajalingam	65	-do-
4.	Venkateshwar Rao	70	-do-
5.	Suryanarayana	65	-do-
6.	Appala Raju	60	-do-
7.	Senigarapu Krishnamurthy	60	-do-
8.	Buggala Rama Rao	65	-do-
XI.	**Chindus :**		
1.	Chindula Yadagiri	70	Nalgonda district
2.	Chindula Ellamma	70	Armour, Nizamabad dist.
3.	Srinivas	55	-do-
4.	Venkataratnam	60	-do-
5.	Rajeshwer	60	-do-
6.	Ballaiah	60	-do-
7.	Neelamma	55	-do-
8.	Susheela	55	-do-
9.	Sammaiah	65	Mucherla, Hanamkonda, Warangal district
10.	Veeraiah	80	-do-
11.	Chindu Nayaka	85	-do-

(Contd.)

(Contd. Appendix-VII)

Sl.	*Name of the Respondents*	*Age*	*Address*
12.	Purushotham	60	-do-
13.	Yellaiah	60	-do-
XII.	**Dakkalis :**		
1.	Karnekanti Hanumanthu	55	Jammikunta, Karimnagar district
2.	Balaswamy	55	Naskal, Warangal district
3.	Gopal	55	-do-
4.	Laxmi	60	-do-
5.	Mutyalamma	60	-do-
6.	Rajulu	48	Parkal, Warangal district.

APPENDIX - VIII

QUESTIONNAIRE

Proforma of the open-ended questionnaire to elicit information from the respondents of Nomadic Tribes.

1. Name :
2. Address :
3. Area of operation :
4. Members of the troupe :
5. Stories :
6. **Visits to Yadava households :**
   - (a) Season :
   - (b) Frequency :
   - (c) Days of normal stay :
   - (d) Details of performance :
   - (e) Earnings :
   - (f) Response from the households :
   - (g) Any other information :
7. **Social status :**
   - (a) Marriage :
   - (b) Family :
   - (c) Community :
   - (d) Customs :
   - (e) Inter-caste relations :
   - (f) Festivals :
   - (g) Any other information :
8. **Economic status :**
   - (a) Houses :
   - (b) Landed property :
   - (c) Animal husbandry :

(d) Main occupation other than this activity :
(e) Income from the visits :
(f) Income from other occupation :
(g) Savings/Borrowings :
(h) Any other information :

9. **Performance :**
(a) Number of stories narrated in one village :
(b) Duration :
(c) Average attendence :
(d) Response from the Audience :
(e) Preservation of manuscripts and family Histories :
(f) Preparation of visual aides and their maintenance :
(g) Involvement of other member of the family :
(h) Any other information :

10. **Present status :**
(a) Historicity :
(b) Patronage :
(c) Attitude of the host community:
(d) Job-satisfaction or otherwise :

Bibliography

PERIODICALS AND GAZETTEERS

Imperial Gazetteers	:	Provincial Series, Hyderabad, 1909.
The Gazetteers of India	:	History and Culture, Department of Culture, 1973.
District Gazetteers	:	Andhra Pradesh, Hyderabad, 1977.
Census of India	:	Andhra Pradesh, Part-II-B, Fairs and Festivals, 1967.
Census of India	:	General Tables British provinces and feudatory states. Vol-II, 1891 and 1931. Madras Presidency, Vol-XV - Caste Index.
Inscriptions of Andhra Pradesh	:	Cuddapah District, Part-I, Government of Andhra Pradesh, Hyderabad, 1977.
Inscriptions of Andhra Pradesh	:	Karimnagar District, Government of Andhra Pradesh, Hyderabad, 1974.

Select Epigraphs of Andhra Pradesh : Government of Andhra Pradesh, Hyderabad, 1965.

A corpus of Inscriptions in the Telangana Districts in Andhra Pradesh, Part-III : Government of Andhra Pradesh, Hyderabad, 1956.

Parabrahma Sastry, P.V. (ed) : Epigraphia Andhrica - Part-IV, Government of Andhra Pradesh, Hyderabad, 1975.

Somasekhara Sharma, M. (ed): Corpus of Telangana Inscriptions, Part-IV, Government of Andhra Pradesh, Hyderabad, 1973.

Venkata Ramanayya, N. (ed) : Epigraphia Andhra - Part-III, Government of Andhra Pradesh, Hyderabad

____________ : Inscriptions of Andhra Pradesh, Warangal District, Government of Andhra Pradesh, Hyderabad, 1974.

KAIFIYATS (Local Records) :

Pattapuravi Kaifiyat : Meckenzie Manuscripts R.No. 1126. Mauje Pattapuravi, Doguru, Narasappanayunipeta, State Archives, Hyderabad

Rana Tikkana Kaifiyat : Descriptive Catalogue of Telugu Dwipada Works, Veturi Prabhakara Sastry, State Archives, Hyderabad

Siddavatam Kaifiyat : Kumbagiri Siddavatam, State Archives, Hyderabad

THESIS (unpublished) :

Mohan Rao, K. : The History of Katamaraju and his times based on palm-leaf manuscripts, Osmania University, Hyderabad, 1990.

Yadagiri Sharma, N. : Janapada Bikshaka Gayakulu, Osmania University, Hyderabad, 1986.

Subba Chary, P. : Janapada Vignanam lo Ashritha Sahityam, Osmania University, Hyderabad, 1992.

Chandraiah, M. : Goudajettila Jeevana Vidanam-Sahityam, Kakatiya University, Warangal, 1999.

ARTICLES :

Arudra : Thappula Thadika Sasanamu, **Bharathi**, Telugu Journal, December, 1960.

Appa Rao, S. : Pothana Padya Sasanamu : Kala nirnaya Samasya, **Bharathi** Telugu Journal, July, 1965.

__________ : Pothana Padya Sasanamu : Kala nirnaya Samasya, **Bharathi**, Telugu Journal, July, 1966.

Brown, C.P. : M/s. No. 1031, 1034, 1040, Published in **Bharathi**, Telugu Journal, May, 1950.

Kodanda Ramaiah, T. : Katamaraju Katha, **Bharathi**, Telugu Journal, May 1953.

__________ : Katamaraju Katha, **Andhra Patrika**, Vijaya Samastradi Sanchika, 1953-54.

Subba Rao, T. : Katamaraju Katha Chakramu, **Bharathi**, Telugu Journal, Jan., 1970.

__________ : Katamaraju Katha Charitraka Samsayamulu, **Bharathi**, Feb., 1971.

__________ : Vira Vidyavanthulu,**Andhra Jyothi**, Jan.,1971.

Venkata Krishna Reddy, D. : Pothana Padya Sasanamu ; Kala nirnaya Samasya, **Bharathi**, March, 1966.

__________ : Katamaraju ; Pullari Yuddakalamu, **Bharathi**, July, 1967.

__________ : Katamaraju ; Pullari Yuddakalamu, Pothana Kalanirnaya Samasya, **Bharathi**, Feb., 1967.

Yeshoda Devi, V. : History of Andhra Country, 100 A.D. to 1500 A.D. subsidiary dynasties, J.A.H.R.S., Vol. XXIII, 1954-56.

BOOKS (English) :

Barbara, Allan. : **The personal point of view in orally communicated History**, Western folklore, 1979.

__________ : **From Memory to History ; Using Oral Sources in Local**

HistoricalResearch, American Association for State and Local History, 1981.

Bavman, Richard. : **Cambridge Studies in Oral and Literate Cultures, story, performance**, London, 1986.

Crooke, W. : **The Tribes and Castes of the North-Western India**, Vol. I to IV, Delhi, 1974.

Carle M. Borden (ed) : **Contemporary India**, Delhi, 1989.

Charlotte I, Lee : **Oral Interpretation**, 2nd Edition, U.S.A., 1959.

Edwin, R.A. Seligman : **Encyclopaedia of the Social Sciences**, Vol. 15, New York, 1935.

Eric, Hobsbawan (ed) : **The Invention of Tradition,** Past and present publication, 1983.

Farqunar, J.N. : **A Primier of Hinduism**, Delhi, 1976.

Finnegan, Ruth : **Oral Poetry,** Cambridge, 1977.

Hoopes, James : **Oral History ; an Introduction for students**, U.S.A., 1980.

Indra Deva : **Folk Culture and Peasant Society in India**, Rawat Publications, 1989.

John, A.C. Boswell. : **Manual of the Nellore District in the Presidency of Madras,** Madras, 1873.

Krishna Rao, B.V. : **History of the Eastern Chalukyas of Vengi** (610-1210 A.D.), Hyderabad 1973.

Kapur, K.D. : **New Atlas of Indian History,** Allahabad, 1953.

Mukerji, Bithika : **The Hindu Tradition,** New York, 1988.

Majumdar, R.C. (ed) : **History and Culture of the Indian people, the Vedic Age,** Vol. I, Bombay, 1952.

Mukunda Rao, N. : **Kalinga Under the Eastern Gangas,** New Delhi, 1988.

Nilakanta Sastry, K.A. : **A History of South India,** 4th edition, Madras, 1984.

Parabrahma Sastry, P.V. : **The Kakatiyas**, Hyderabad, 1978.

Rameshan, N. : **The Eastern Chalukyas of Vengi,** Hyderabad, 1975.

Richard, M. Dorson (ed) : **Folklore and Folklife, an introduction,** London, 1972.

Russell, R.V. : **The Tribes and Castes of the Central Provinces of India,** Delhi, 1975.

Sherring, M.A. : **Hindu Tribes and Castes,** Vol. II, Delhi, 1974.

Swamikhannu Pillai, L.D. : **Indian Ephemeris,** Madras, 1922.

Sherwani, H.K. : **History of Medieval Deccan,** Hyderabad, 1973.

Siraj-ul-Hassan, Syed. : **Castes and Tribes of H.E.H., The Nizam's Dominions,** New Delhi, 1920.

Suryanarayana, Kolluru. : **History of the Minor Chalukya Families in Medieval Andhradesa,** Delhi, 1986.

__________ : **Feudatories under Eastern Chalukyas** Delhi, 1987.

Stith Thomson and Jonas Balyas. : **The Oral Tales of India,** Indiana University, 1958.

Thurston, Edgar. : **Castes and Tribes of Southern India,** Delhi, 1909.

Jan Vansina : **Oral Tradition ; A Study of Historical Methodology,** London, 1965.

Vijaya, N. : **The role of Traditional Folk media in Rural areas,** Hyderabad, 1985.

Venkata Ramanaiah, N. : **The Chalukyas of Vengi,** Madras, 1950.

Vladimir, Propp. : **Theory and History of Folklore,** U.S.A., 1984.

O'flaherty, Wendy Doniger (ed) : **Textual Sources for the Study of Hinduism,** Manchester, 1988.

Walter J. Ong. : **Orality and literacy,** U.S.A., 1963.

Yazdani, G. (ed) : **The early History of the Deccan,** Parts VII, XI, Bombay, 1960.

BOOKS (TELUGU) :

Arudra : **Samagrandhra Sahitya Charitra,** Kakatiya Yugam, Vol.2, Madras, 1965.

Aruna Kumari, B. : **Andhra Vangmayamuna Charitraka Kavyamulu,** Vishakhapatnam, 1978.

Balendu Shekharam, K. : **Andhrula Charitra,** Rajahmundry, 1961.

Bala Rama Murthy, A. : **Andhrula Samkshipta Charitra,** Vijayawada, 1953.

Chandra Sekhara Reddy, N. (ed): **Vikrama Simhapuri Mandala Sarvasamu,** Nellore, 1963.

Dronappa, Thumati. : **Janapada Kala Sampada,** Hyderabad, 1972.

Deviprasad Yadav, Malyala : **Yadava Chandrika,** Hyderabad, 1982.

Gangappa, S. : **Jathiki Prathibimbam Janapada Sahityam,** 1984.

Gurubrahma Sarma, M. : **Kondaveeti Samrajam,** Guntur, 1920.

Hanumantha Rao, B.S.L. : **Andhrula Charitra,** Guntur, 1983.

Ramaiah Panthulu, Jayanthi. : **Sri Suryarayandra Nighanttuvu,** Vol. VI, Hyderabad, 1982.

Krishna Kumari, Nayani : **Telugu Janapada Geyagathalu,** Hyderabad, 1977.

__________ : **Janapada Sahitya Charitra,** Hyderabad, 1976.

Laxmiranjanam, K. : **Andhrula Charitra-Samskruti,** Kurnool, 1965.

Lakshmaiah, B. : **Rajavamsha Pradipika,** 2nd edition, Tenali, 1958.

Lakshmi Kantham, Pingali : **Andhra Sahitya Chritra,** Hyderabad, 1976.

__________ : **Palnati Veera Charitra,** Hyderabad, 1976.

Mohan, G.S. : **Janapada Kathalu,** Secunderabad, 1984.

__________ : **Janapadula Nammakalu,** Ananthapuram, 1983.

__________ : **Samethalalo Sanghika Jeevanam,** Ananthapuram, 1981.

__________ : **Janapada Vignana Vyasavali,** Ananthapuram, 1981.

Nagaiah, G. : **Telugu Sahitya Samiksha,** Tirupati, 1985.

Narayanamatya, A. : **Hamsavimsati,** Hyderabad, 1977.

Pratapa Reddy, S. : **Andhrula Sanghika Charitra,** Hyderabad, 1949.

Pratap, D.R. : **Tribal of Andhra Pradesh,** 1975.

Prabhakara Sastri, V. (ed) : **Katamaraju Katha, Madras,** 1953.

Premalatha, R. : **Telugu Janapada Sahityamu,** Puragathalu, Hyderabad, 1983.

Premalatha, R. & Sri Laxmi, K. : **Janapada Vignana Parisheelanam Vyasa Sankalanam,** Hyderabad, 1990.

Radhakrishna Murthy, M. : **Andhrula Nataka Ranga Charitra**, Hyderabad, 1974.

Ramaraju, B. : **Telugu Janapada Geya Sahityamu,** Hyderabad, 1978.

Rama Rao, M. (ed) : **Kakatiya Sanchika,** Rajahmahendravaram, 1935.

Rangacharyulu, C. : **Andhra Shabda Ratnakaram,** Eluru, 1984.

Radhakrishna, Budaraju. : **Pracheenandhra Sasanamulu,** Hyderabad, 1971.

Radhakrishna Murthy, M. : **Teluguvari Janapada Kala Rupalu,** Hyderabad, 1992.

Ramakrishnamacharya, Nanduri. : **Pracheena Dakshina Bharatha Charitra,** Guntur, 1967.

Ramakrishna Sharma, : **Telangana Sasanamulu,** Vol-II, Gadiyaram (ed) Hyderabad, 1960.

Ramaiah Panthulu, : **Sasana Padya Manjari,** Kakinada, 1961.

__________ : **Suryarayandhra Nighanttuvu,** Kakinada, 1944.

Sri Rama Appa Rao, P. : **Telugu Nataka Vikasamu,** Hyderabad, 1967.

Satyanarayana, K. : **Andhrula Samskruthi-Charitra,** Vol-II, Hyderabad, 1982.

Subramanyam, G.V. : **Purana Vagmayam,** Hyderabad, 1975.

Satyanarayana, : **Sri Kanyaka Puranam,** Vijayawada,1986.

Sundaram, R.V.S. : **Janapada Sahityam,** Secunderabad, 1982.

Somana, Palkuriki. : **Basavapuranam,** Andhra Grandhamala, 1952.

__________ : **Panditharadya Charitra,** Chennapuri, 1974.

Susheela, T. : **Andhra Dwipada Sahitya Charitra,** Delhi, 1979.

Satyavathi, Tella. : **Telugu Vari intiperlu,** Guntur, 1987.

Seshaiah, Chaganti. : **Andhra Kavitarangini,** Vol. I, East Godavari, 1961.

Somasekhara Sarma, M. : **Vignana Sarvasvam,** Vol. IV, Madras, 1961.

Shyamala Sastri, Kotra. (ed) : **Andhra Vachaspatyamu,** Madras, 1959.

Virabhadra Rao, Chilukuri. : **Andhrula Charitram,** Vignana Chadrika, Book Depot, 1912.

Venkatarangaiah, M. : **Sangraha Andhra Vignana Kosam,** Vol.III, Hyderabad, 1962.

Venkateshwara Gupta, T. : **Sri Vasavi Kanyaka Purana Sangraha Sachitramu,** Penugonda, 1984.

Venkata Subba Rao, T. : **Katamaraju Kathalu,** Vol. I, Hyderabad, 1976.

Venkata Laxmana Rao : **Hindu Desa Katha Sangrahamu,** Chennapuri, 1908.

Vijaya Bharathi : **Telugu Sahitya Koshamu,** Hyderabad, 1980.

Vira Raghavacharyulu, K. : **Vishwa Karma Puranam,** Tenali, 1986.

Index

H

I

J

K

L

M

N

O

P

T

U

V

W

Y